THE CULT FILES

THE CULT FILES

HISTORY'S MOST MYSTERIOUS SECTS AND SOCIETIES REVEALED

LEO MOYNIHAN & SAM PILGER

NEW BURLINGTON

This edition first published in 2023 by
New Burlington Books,
1 Triptych Place, London, SE1 9SH, United Kingdom.

ISBN 978-1-80242-091-3

Conceived, designed, and produced by
The Bright Press, an imprint of the Quarto Group,
1 Triptych Place, London,
SE1 9SH, United Kingdom.
T (0)20 7700 6700
www.Quarto.com

Printed in China

10 9 8 7 6 5 4 3 2 1

CONTENTS

Introduction **6**

1

VIOLENCE AND MURDER 8

Peoples Temple **10**
Branch Davidians **16**
Colonia Dignidad **22**
The Manson Family **28**
Aum Shinrikyo **34**
Order of the Solar Temple **40**
Movement for the Restoration
of the Ten Commandments of
God **46**

2

NUDISM, ABUSE, AND SEXUAL EXPLOITATION 52

The Freedomites **54**
The Sullivanians **60**
Children of God **66**
Ant Hill Kids **72**
Angel's Landing **78**
Sarah Lawrence College Cult **84**

3

FUNDAMENTALIST CULTS 88

Unification Church **90**
FLDS **96**
School of Prophets **102**
The Kirtland Cult **108**
True Russian Orthodox Church **114**

4

CONSPIRACY AND NEW AGE 120

NXIVM **122**
Aetherius Society **128**
Nuwaubian Nation **134**
The Family **140**
The Brethren **146**
Love Has Won **150**
Heaven's Gate **156**

5

ECCENTRIC AND WEIRD 160

The Prince Philip Movement **162**
Synanon **166**
Eckankar **172**
Church of Bible Understanding **176**
Universal Medicine **180**

Further Reading **186**
Index **188**
Credits **192**

INTRODUCTION

The word "cult" stems from the Latin *cultus*, meaning "care, cultivation, worship." Their leaders will promise such things, and people have long been drawn to the comfort that they imagine will exist within. But are these groups always what they seem? The word "cult" more often conjures up the image of brainwashed fanatics following a charismatic but dangerous leader.

The modern cult has intrigued, frightened, and repelled observers for decades. Ever since the counterculture of the 1960s, people (mainly the younger generation in search of both independence and belonging) have been attracted to alternative ways of thinking, ways of "bettering themselves," all within a community that goes against the status quo.

While some groups will argue that their work has offered all of that in an innocent way, there can be no doubting that over the last seventy years, dangerous cults have become increasingly prevalent, and their leaders have become as notorious as any hardened criminals.

Charming, charismatic, attractive leaders such as Jim Jones and Keith Raniere have been able to "recruit" in large numbers, offering supposed enlightenment but in turn receiving vast amounts of money and sex, some even persuading followers that the only way to salvation is death. Manipulation is the most important tool these leaders possess. In *The Cult Files* we will examine how leaders such as Jim Jones exert total control over their followers. Having convinced members of his Peoples Temple to separate themselves from their family, their past lives, and society, Jones was then able to use humiliation and paranoia to ultimately cause mass suicide. Such brutality is alarmingly common. We will put these cases under the spotlight and look at how these dangerous leaders have brought tragic ends to so many devoted followers. By looking at cases such as the notorious Charles Manson and his murderous "Family" and the Japanese cult leader Shoko

Asahara, we will examine how these men convinced their followers to kill innocent people.

If murder is the extreme, cults and their leaders have long held other similarly disturbing motivations, and this book will examine how sex and sexual abuse is so often a byproduct of cult membership. We look at Lou Castro, in his Angels Landing commune, who was able to convince followers that he had to have sex or he would die, and Roch Thériault, the leader of the Ant Hill Kids cult who fathered twenty-six children.

Religion is often used to entice members with divine hope and the promise of spiritual enlightenment. In Russia, the True Orthodox Church broke away from mainstream religion in 2007 with dangerous consequences, and Ron Lafferty's fundamentalist Mormon church ended with tragic results in 1984. New Age religion is also prevalent, and we will focus on movements such as Australia's The Family and America's Aetherius Society.

Cults don't have to mean danger, abuse, and death. Many have offered simpler, more innocent incentives, perhaps none more so than the Prince Philip movement in the South Pacific that worshipped the UK's Duke of Edinburgh. As *The Cult Files* proves, these groups take many different forms.

1

VIOLENCE
AND
MURDER

While most cults recruit their
followers with the promise of
peace, love, and harmony, in
reality they often descend into
violence and murder. We look
at seven cults that witnessed
shocking body counts, including
the mass suicide of 913 followers
of the Peoples Temple in 1978,
the burned bodies of fifty-three
followers of the Order of the
Solar Temple who killed themselves
in 1994, and the fire and botched
raid on the Branch Davidians'
Texas compound that led to the
deaths of seventy-six of their
followers in 1993.

PEOPLES

TEMPLE

LOCATION:............................... USA AND GUYANA

YEARS ACTIVE:.. 1955-78

FOUNDER:... JIM JONES

A captivating preacher committed to racial integration and social change, Jim Jones convinced his congregation to follow him from Indiana to California, then into the jungle in Guyana. At first, his compelling sermons and seemingly socially progressive motives attracted many dedicated followers, but when his Peoples Temple came under the spotlight, Jones's true character came to the fore, resulting in terror and tragedy on an unimaginable scale.

Jim Jones was born in Crete, Indiana, in May 1931. He grew up in the neighboring town of Lynn as part of a poor family, with a sickly father and neglectful mother, who lived in a rundown shack. Despite his challenging upbringing, Jones always had a strong belief in himself. When he was nine years old he told his school classmates he had superpowers and could fly, but only succeeded in breaking his arm when he leaped off a roof.

At an early age, Jones developed a strong interest in religion and politics, stating his desire to become a preacher. Ignored by his family, with few friends, he took himself to services at the local Pentecostal church. "I was a poor child, who lived on the wrong side of the tracks," he said. "I became sensitive to the feelings of Blacks as they weren't accepted like me, and it was at the Pentecostal church that I finally found some love."

After graduating from university and marrying Marceline Baldwin, Jones was able to devote himself to his passions of religion and social change. He began to travel across Indiana and Ohio, honing his flamboyant style and preaching to congregations about the need to challenge the evil of capitalism and the racial segregation that was still prevalent in 1950s America.

A NEW CHURCH

After moving between several churches across the Midwest as a student pastor, Jones was given the chance as an ordained minister to establish a new church in Indianapolis, Indiana, in 1955, which he called Peoples Temple. He started with only twenty members, but the church soon grew in popularity as word spread about Jones's

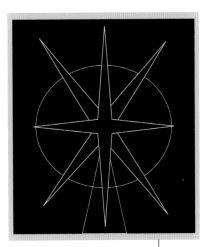

The logo of the Peoples Temple appeared on the group's pamphlets and promotional materials.

mesmerizing and inspiring sermons. Jones spoke about the issues of race and class and the need for fundamental change, a message that resonated with the poor and disenfranchised.

"He had charisma and presence, and he was handsome, and had a fire in his eyes, even when he wore sunglasses," his son Stephan said.

In Indiana at a time when the Ku Klux Klan was still active, Jones insisted his congregation was integrated, and demanded that Black and white Americans come together. Jones and Marceline themselves created a "rainbow family," adopting sons of Native-American, Korean-American, and African-American descent.

The Peoples Temple offered more than just church services; it reached out to the community with a soup kitchen, a medical clinic, a day care center for children, drug rehabilitation for addicts, and help for the homeless.

MOVE TO CALIFORNIA

By 1965, Jones wanted to reach a wider audience and moved his church to Redwood Valley in California. Around 150 of his congregation followed him to a plot of land just over 100 miles (160 kilometers) north of San Francisco, where they lived and worked together to create an egalitarian, utopian Christian community. Jones said he chose the location as the perfect place to survive nuclear fall-out.

Jones began to specialize in faith healing, claiming he could heal the sick, but it was all a con. He once got a follower to sit in a wheelchair and pretend he had suddenly made her walk and run again in front of a crowd that went wild. His followers began to believe he had the powers of a god.

In 1971, Jones moved his church to San Francisco, with an outpost in Los Angeles, becoming a political force who could provide followers for rallies and help secure votes for local and state politicians. But the move brought his church into the spotlight, and within a year, the *San Francisco Examiner* had run a story stating Jones was a false messiah who claimed to have brought forty-three people back from the dead. The following year, scrutiny intensified when eight followers left his church and publicly complained about his mind control and abuse (see Case Notes, page 15).

JONESTOWN

As the pressure grew in the USA, Jones sought a way out by purchasing 27,000 acres (109 square kilometers) near Matthew Ridge in Guyana and moving his church there to create what would become known as Jonestown. In 1975, the first fifty people arrived to begin building the town, and by 1977, they had established a community of nearly a thousand followers.

At first there was a sense of optimism. The followers thought they were building a socialist utopia in the jungle; some felt they had found a promised land. But discontent soon took hold as they began to feel overworked and underfed, and some referred to it as a "slave plantation" where they were forced to listen to Jones deliver his sermons through a megaphone as they worked in the fields.

Concerned relatives of Jones's followers back in the USA began to raise the alarm about life in Guyana, saying it was more like a concentration camp with armed guards, where they were brainwashed and forced into working, with their passports confiscated to stop them leaving. In August 1977, *New*

Jones moved his followers to dense jungle near the Venezuelan border.

West magazine published an article alleging Jones was a charlatan who beat his followers and was guilty of financial mismanagement.

California Congressman Leo Ryan announced he would undertake a fact-finding mission to Jonestown accompanied by a TV crew from NBC News. The occupants of the settlement had been primed by Jones to express their happiness to Ryan, and threatened with punishment if they strayed from an agreed script. At first Ryan was enchanted by what he saw. On the second day, however, he was attacked with a knife but was unharmed, and several followers came forward to ask if they could return to the USA with him.

The following afternoon Ryan and his entourage left early, with fourteen followers who wished to defect, for a flight at the local Kaituma airstrip. While waiting for their two small aircraft, the group came under fire from loyal Peoples Temple members. Ryan (who was hit by more than twenty bullets), three journalists, and a defecting Temple member were all killed, and nine others wounded.

When Jones learned of the killings back at the settlement, he told them the government would now annihilate the town and torture their children. He said the only possible response was to commit "mass revolutionary suicide" to protest against an inhumane world. "We've had as much of this world as you're going to get," he told them. "Let's just be done with it, let's be done with the agony of it."

On the morning of November 19, 1978, a group of Guyanese troops were greeted with a scene of unimaginable horror when they arrived in Jonestown. They found a collection of 913 dead bodies, a third of them children. It was the biggest ever loss of civilian life in a deliberate act in US history. Jones himself was also found dead with what appeared to be a self-inflicted gunshot wound.

Jones had served a lethal punch of Flavor Aid (later misidentified as Kool-Aid) and cyanide to his followers gathered at the main church building. It was described as a mass suicide, but the children who died did not make this decision for themselves, and there was also evidence that up to seventy people had been forcibly injected with the poison.

Jones was a murderous cult leader responsible for the deaths of 913 of his followers.

CASE NOTES:
CONMAN WITH A DARK SIDE

At the start of the 1970s, Jones wanted to assert greater control over his congregation. He wanted to be called "Father" and be seen as a godlike figure who could control their bank accounts and housing deeds. He sought to alienate them from their families and keep them inside his church. He would sometimes beat his followers if they threatened to leave, or disappointed him in any way.

"He was a predator who mastered the art of luring people in from every segment of life," former follower Yulanda Williams said.

Jones would have sex with his followers, both male and female, and he also used drugs. "A lot of my father's craziness was kept well-hidden for a lot of years," said his son Stephan. "He was as nuts as anyone . . . a sick, demented child in a man's body."

BRANCH

DAVIDIANS

LOCATION:.......................... WACO, TEXAS, USA

YEARS ACTIVE:..................................... 1934-93

FOUNDER:.............................. VICTOR HOUTEFF

A religious group had been under siege for fifty-one days, with a leader who proclaimed he was the second coming of Christ, and that the armed federal and military agents outside were bringing the end of days. Several deaths had already occurred during the dreadful standoff, but then the armed forces moved in. Gunfire, tanks, helicopters, and then a fire that killed almost eighty followers of the Branch Davidians. Who were they and why had this tragedy happened?

Excommunicated by the Seventh-Day Adventist Church, Houteff moved his family to Texas and founded the Davidians.

In 1929, Victor Houteff, a Bulgarian immigrant living in southern California, broke away from his Seventh-Day Adventist (SDA) Church. An SDA school teacher, the church leaders opposed Houteff's interpretation of parts of the Bible and the fact that he claimed to be a living prophet sent from God.

Houteff and many members of his Bible class were asked to leave, so having moved himself and his followers to Waco, Texas, in 1934, he set up a commune. Now called the Davidians, the group studied the Bible and took its words as literal truth. Their focus was the Book of Revelations and the Seven Seals, which they believed to be God's sequence of events leading to the "Judgement Day" that will only be explained by a "Lamb of God" who will come during the last days.

When Houteff died in 1954, his wife struggled to keep the sect going. In 1959, a man named Benjamin Roden reformed the group, calling it the Branch Davidians. When he died in 1978, his wife Lois took charge, and while she clashed with her son George Roden over the rightful leadership, she had taken a young man named Vernon Howell under her tutelage.

Howell had lived a hard life, being passed between his mother (and her violent partners) and his grandparents. Being dyslexic, he had struggled to settle at school, where kids nicknamed him "Mr. Retardo," but having enrolled at a private SDA school, the musical and now charismatic young man, already able to recite the Old and New Testament by heart, became fascinated by prophecy. Having joined in 1981, and learning under Lois, Howell's influence upon the Branch Davidians grew. When Lois died in 1986, Howell laid claims to be the group's rightful new leader despite the opposition of her son George.

A NEW LEADER

George Roden and Vernon Howell's rivalry spilled over into an armed confrontation at the group's headquarters at Mount Carmel near Waco in 1987, when Howell and seven followers raided the center with rifles and shotguns. Roden had exhumed the dead body of a former member, and while he claimed he had done so merely to relocate the community cemetery, Howell told a subsequent trial that Roden had challenged him to "raise the dead" as way of deciding the leadership, and that by coming to the center, he had simply sought photographic evidence. The trial was thrown out, Howell and his followers were acquitted, and when Roden was convicted of murder in 1989 (he claimed his victim had been sent to kill him by Howell), leaving an array of debts, Howell and his followers raised the arrears and moved into Mount Carmel, with Howell now as ultimate leader.

In May 1990, Howell legally changed his name to David Koresh. David from the Bible's King David, from whom a Messiah would come, and Koresh, the Hebrew word for Cyrus, as in Cyrus the Great, a Persian king who freed the Jews in Babylon. Koresh enjoyed great success as the Branch Davidians' leader. His vast knowledge of the Bible, the Revelations' Seven Seals in particular, drew swathes of new members to Mount Carmel. They came from all walks of life, multiracial and international, and they worked locally to fund their religious way of life.

Koresh continued to talk about himself as a new Christ, describing the group as "students of the Seven Seals." He claimed that there was a pending attack on the Branch Davidians by apocalyptic outside forces, and so more weapons

A seemingly normal family: Vernon Wayne Howell (aka David Koresh) with his wife, Rachel, and son, Cyrus, outside their home in 1986.

were obtained. Not only were the group becoming more weaponized, but rumors of emotional, physical, and sexual abuse began to materialize. As their leader and prophet, Koresh was said to control the lives of his followers and their children. He controlled what they ate, he ordered severe beatings of the children, often until they bled. He demanded celibacy for everyone except himself and his "wives," as he was, according to the scriptures, to have twenty-four pure children who one day would rule "a new Eden."

It was allegations of the sexual abuse of the group's children and growing concerns about the stockpiling of weaponry that initially attracted the attention of the press, and then brought in the law enforcers. The end of days was indeed coming.

DEADLY SIEGE

When the *Waco Tribune-Herald* ran a story in February 1993 headlined "The Sinful Messiah," details about activities within the group shocked readers. Claims of statutory rape, underage brides, and Koresh fathering multiple children from wives as young as 12 drew attention to the possible wrongdoings that were taking place. The local sheriff later claimed he had looked into these claims but could find no proof. However, when a delivery driver informed his office that a package had opened revealing firearms and ammunition, he notified the Bureau of Alcohol, Tobacco, and Firearms (ATF). Supporters of Koresh and the group claimed it as their constitutional right

A shocked nation watched as the Mount Carmel Center in Waco was engulfed in flames.

to own those weapons, but with further investigation, the ATF suspected that guns were being modified and illegal automatic weapons were being held. On February 28, their officials ordered a raid on the property.

Agents hoped for the element of surprise and a peaceful search of the property. They got neither. En route to the raid, a television news crew asked a local postman for directions to Mount Carmel. That postman happened to be Koresh's brother-in-law, who tipped off the cult leader. A two-hour gun battle followed. As agents and group members exchanged intense fire, nine people were killed (four agents and five Davidians), before a fifty-day standoff ensued. In one of his siege videos, Koresh said, "You come pointing guns in the direction of my wives and my kids, dammit, I'll meet you at the door anytime. I'm sorry some of you guys got shot, but hey, God will have to sort that out won't he?"

Weeks of negotiations followed. Tourists flocked to the area. Some children were released, but many wanted to stay. FBI negotiators were said to be alarmed at the intensity of the members' religious devotion, and realized that to them, this was an apocalyptic event. Koresh continued to state that the federal and military presence signaled the "end of times" event he had predicted. Fearing a mass suicide, on April 19, federal agents once again began to raid the compound, using CS gas, explosives, and tanks to try to force members out and aid an evacuation. No Davidians left.

At noon, a fire broke out. As the country watched live on television, the fire took hold and within the compound walls, seventy-eight people (including Koresh) died, many of them children. The FBI claimed that the fire was started by the inhabitants; later some surviving Davidians claimed it was started by the agents' explosives.

The question of who was to blame in Waco has raged on. In 2000, a jury found federal agents not liable for the deaths that day, and while five surviving Branch Davidians were found guilty of firearm charges, they were released in 2007. After the siege, splinter groups of the Branch Davidians appeared, and one, called "The Branch, The Lord Our Righteousness," continues to await the resurrection of David Koresh.

CASE NOTES: THE OKLAHOMA BOMBING

On April 19, 1995 (two years to the day after the Waco fire), a truck bomb attack in Oklahoma killed 168 people. When arrested, its perpetrator, Timothy McVeigh, stated that he had traveled to Waco to protest the federal government's treatment of the Branch Davidians, and as part of an antigovernment militia movement, he had sought revenge for what happened at Mount Carmel. To this day, the bombing remains America's deadliest act of domestic terrorism.

COLONIA
DIGNIDAD

LOCATION:......................MAULE REGION, CHILE

YEARS ACTIVE:...1961-96

FOUNDER:...............................PAUL SCHÄFER

A former Nazi founded a remote colony where for over three decades he brainwashed his followers, routinely sexually abused children, and performed torture in underground chambers. The colony became almost an autonomous state under the leadership of Paul Schäfer, a preacher and former Nazi who had served in World War II. It was also home to around 300 indoctrinated Germans and a sanctuary for Nazi fugitives and the dictatorial regime of General Pinochet, who tortured hundreds of opponents there.

Former Nazi Paul Schäfer founded a colony in Chile that became known as a "pedophile's paradise."

Schäfer was born in 1921 in the town of Troisdorf, near Bonn, and as a young man was fitted with a glass eye after an accident with a fork. He worked as a medic for the Nazis in World War II at a field hospital in occupied France. After the war he became a young people's leader in the Evangelical Free Church but was fired after being accused of sexually abusing boys. He then embarked on a career as a preacher, touring Germany and spreading the word of the US minister William Branham, who believed in faith healing, racial purity, women's submission to men, and an impending apocalypse.

During the 1950s Schäfer established a community in Gronau, Germany, and set up a children's home in nearby Siegburg for widows arriving from East Prussia. But in 1959, he was charged with sexually abusing two boys and a warrant was issued for his arrest. Schäfer needed to get out of the country and it was at this point he made plans to move the community to Chile.

In 1961, Schäfer's colony of German immigrants, Colonia Dignidad ("Dignity Colony"), was established on the banks of the Perquilauquen River in the Maule Region of central Chile, 230 miles (370 kilometers) south of the capital Santiago. Amid the lush landscape and winding rivers, it appeared an idyllic location but in fact became the site of numerous horrific crimes, including forced labor, murders, sadistic torture, and the ritual sexual abuse of children.

In 2019, a report commissioned by the German government said Schäfer "tore families apart, abused countless children, and actively collaborated with Pinochet henchmen on torture, murder, and disappearances . . . The survivors still suffer massively from the severe psychological and physical consequences after years of harm caused by violence, abuse, exploitation, and slave labor."

DESTRUCTION OF FAMILIES

In the years after World War II, a ravaged Germany was a bleak and hopeless country, with people looking for a cause to follow, a role preachers came to fulfill. Perhaps this is why, when in 1961, Schäfer told his congregation the Russians were coming to occupy Germany and they should follow him to Chile to set up a new colony, 300 people answered his call.

Schäfer's followers believed they were creating a happy Christian colony celebrating hard work, discipline, and community. The colony boasted a farm, a bakery, a chapel, two schools, a power station, highly profitable mills and factories, and a free medical center that offered care to the colony and the surrounding local population.

Schäfer's vision was to create a community where families did not exist. To this end he separated families and put people into groups organized by age and gender. There were four groups: The Babies, from birth; The Wedges, from 15 years old; The Elder Servants, from 30 years old; and The Comalos, from 50 years upward.

Children were taken from their parents at birth and raised in a communal nursery. They were not allowed to know who their parents were. All adults were simply known as "Uncles" or "Aunts," with Schäfer known as "The Permanent Uncle." The children were denied a normal family life, and were instead put to work without pay in the fields of the colony. "I started work when I was seven years old," former member Winfried Hempel has said. "It was every day, from early in the morning to late at night, with delayed meals, few hours of sleep, and forced labor. Those who didn't obey were beaten, locked up, and punished."

ABUSE AND TORTURE

Separating children from their parents also allowed Schäfer to sexually abuse them with impunity. "The abuse of children at Colonia Dignidad was a ritualized, organized, and perfected practice; it was a pedophile's paradise," lawyer Hernan Fernandez, who represented some of the victims, has said. "These children had no protection as families did not exist . . . and he [Schäfer] sometimes abused three or four boys on the same day."

The colony was secured
with locked gates and
a barbed-wire fence,
to prevent any escapes.

No children were spared, even those whose parents were in Schäfer's inner circle, and if any resisted his advances they were taken to a building where experiments were carried out to suppress sexual instincts. Screams could be heard as boys were punished with an electric cattle prod used on their testicles or were attacked by dogs.

The abuse and control continued as Schäfer instilled in his followers a fear of the devil and communism, telling them they would only ever be safe if they stayed with him at the colony. They were cut off from the outside world, and were denied newspapers, television, radios, and use of a telephone. Leaving was also difficult, as the colony was surrounded by a fence with barbed wire, a watch tower, motion sensors, and cameras hidden in trees.

In 1977, Amnesty International reported on the colony's torture, but no action was taken, and in 1984, three of Schäfer's aides managed to escape and return to Germany, where they raised the alarm with accusations of slavery and violence. By 1990, General Pinochet's dictatorship came to an end and the return of democracy steadily removed the colony's protection.

EXPOSED

Over this time, the colony's population declined, and to survive, Schäfer opened up membership to the local population. He decided to establish the Intensive Boarding School, but in 1995, one of its students, a 12-year-old boy, passed a note to his mother which read: "Take me out of here. He raped me." A doctor confirmed the boy had been raped, which prompted the mother to avoid the potentially corrupt local police and take her complaint straight to the Chief of National Detectives, Luis Henriquez, in the capital Santiago. When a warrant was issued for Schäfer's arrest in 1996, he fled the country and disappeared.

In Schäfer's absence, Henriquez found a cache of incriminating files, a series of graves, and a stockpile of arms and weapons, including rocket launchers and a dangerous amount of the lethal nerve agent sarin, which had been produced there for the deposed Pinochet regime.

Life at the colony continued but without the same brutality as under Schäfer, who remained free until he was finally tracked down in 2005, hiding out in a townhouse on the edge of the Argentine capital Buenos Aires. A year later, after being extradited back to Chile, Schäfer was convicted of child abuse and

Victims' families placed placards next to a grave where murdered cult members were buried and later exhumed.

sentenced to twenty years in prison, but he only served four before he died of heart failure in April 2010, at the age of 88.

Today the colony remains open as the rebranded Villa Baviera, a holiday resort inviting tourists to experience a slice of Germany in Chile, with a themed restaurant and rooms. There are still some former colonists who live on the grounds as it is the only home they have ever known.

In 2019, a government commission in Germany agreed to pay compensation of €10,000 ($10,500) to each of the colony's remaining victims. However, many of them believed this was not nearly enough. "[It] covers very little, if you compare it to the forty years of work without pay," said Horst Schaffrick, who lived there, and also referred to "the suffering caused by slavery, beatings, drugs, and sexual abuse."

CASE NOTES:
DICTATORSHIP AND FUGITIVE SANCTUARY

In September 1973, Chile's democratically elected President Salvador Allende was overthrown in a bloody coup by General Augusto Pinochet. In this new era Schäfer reached out to offer help to the new military dictatorship in return for continued protection for his colony.

Schäfer allowed Pinochet's forces to use the colony's torture chambers to interrogate political opponents. It is estimated 300 people were tortured there, sometimes by Schäfer himself, most with electric shocks inside their bodies. As many as a hundred were murdered, their bodies placed in mass graves at the colony, which were later dug up and burned or dropped in the sea.

The colony also became a sanctuary for Nazi fugitives who were on the run in South America, including Josef Mengele, a former SS officer known as the "Angel of Death" for performing experiments on prisoners at Auschwitz, and another SS officer Walter Rauff, who was responsible for 100,000 deaths as the inventor of the mobile gas chambers.

THE MANSON FAMILY

LOCATION:.. LOS ANGELES, CALIFORNIA, USA

YEARS ACTIVE:.................................. 1967-75

FOUNDER:............................. CHARLES MANSON

The Manson Family was created by Charles Manson, a creepy but charismatic drifter and aspiring musician who inspired such blind devotion during the late 1960s that his followers were prepared to obey him without question. His disciples, mostly young women, were lured into his extended family at a ranch where they followed his every command, even if it involved the brutal murders of innocent people.

Born in Cincinnati, Ohio, in 1934, to a 15-year-old single mother, Manson endured a chaotic and abusive childhood, moving around the country living with various family members after his mother was jailed. Manson spent time in foster care and homes for juvenile delinquents, where he claimed he was raped by other students, and often tried to escape. At the age of 14 he robbed a grocery store, which marked the start of a life of petty crime where he was continually in and out of jail. He also worked as a pimp, got married, and had a son.

Members of the Family
in a 1973 documentary,
with Manson himself
bottom left.

When Manson was released from jail in March 1967, aged 32, he moved to San Francisco at the height of the "Summer of Love," when Haight-Ashbury was the focal point of the counter-culture movement. He moved into the apartment of 23-year-old librarian Mary Brunner and persuaded her to let eighteen other women join them. Manson used the free-love spirit of the times, fueled by drug use, to target vulnerable women and lure them into what would soon become a cult.

"This sexual freedom provided opportunity for women to be abused or taken advantage of," said former member of the Family Dianne Lake.

"He took girls and remolded them," said follower Leslie van Houten. "I wanted more living out of life than was expected for young girls at that time, like drugs and sex, and breaking away from the norm. For as twisted as it got, I thought [Charles] had the answers, and I had met someone who by being around them would make a positive change."

A naturally manipulative character, Manson soon had around a hundred followers. In 1968 they moved to Los Angeles, at first living with Dennis Wilson of the Beach Boys. Manson hoped Wilson could help him get a recording contract, allowing his followers to have sex with him in return.

After being evicted from Wilson's house, the Manson Family moved to the Spahn Ranch, thirty minutes from Los Angeles, used as a set for Western movies and TV shows. Manson demanded his followers give away their watches and have no sense of time, and consent to his every command. This would include sex with him or the owner of the ranch.

"I like women, they are nice and soft and put together well," Manson said in an interview from prison in 1981. "Just as long as they keep their mouths shut and do what they are supposed to. That is the extent of it. All this occult, hocus pocus [stuff] is a fairytale."

Manson's embrace of religion and his philosophy were simply a means to attract attention and control women. As Aja Romano wrote for *Vox* in 2019, "This narrative of Manson has thankfully diminished over time, and given way to the truth: that beneath all his theatrics, his bizarre ramblings, his googly-eyed camera-hogging, and his violent outbursts, Manson's evil wasn't outsize, occult, or supernatural. He was an average, everyday narcissist who practiced social engineering and learned to use the bodies of willing women around him as a bargaining tool."

"Manson, who was uneducated but highly intelligent, had this phenomenal ability to gain control over other people and get them to do terrible things," said former Los Angeles District Attorney Vincent Bugliosi, who prosecuted him. "Eventually he convinced them that he was the second coming: Christ and the Devil all wrapped up in the same person."

A MURDEROUS AND BLOODY SPREE

Manson used this control to lead his followers on a bloody killing spree throughout Los Angeles during the summer of 1969. On July 25, Manson sent followers Brunner, Bobby Beausoleil, and Susan Atkins to the Topanga Canyon apartment of Gary Allen Hinman, a PhD student at UCLA. He believed Hinman had inherited money and wanted him to join the Family.

The Manson Family murdered five people at a mansion in the Benedict Canyon area of Los Angeles in August 1969.

Hinman was held hostage for two days. Manson arrived and slashed his face, before ordering Beausoleil to stab him to death. The women wrote "Political piggy" and drew a paw print in the victim's blood to implicate the Black revolutionary group the Black Panthers. Ten days later, Beausoleil was arrested driving Hinman's car with the murder weapon inside. The following year, he was convicted of first-degree murder and sentenced to life in prison.

Meanwhile, Manson had a taste for more. On August 8, 1969, he sent four followers—Atkins, Tex Watson, Linda Kasabian, and Patricia Krenwinkel—to 10050 Cielo Drive, Los Angeles, to "totally destroy" everyone and do it "as gruesome as you can." The address was the home of actress Sharon Tate, wife of movie director Roman Polanski, who was enjoying an evening in with her friends: hairstylist Jay Sebring, screenwriter Wojciech Frykowski, and heiress Abigail Folger.

The Manson followers arrived just after midnight and killed 18-year-old Steven Parent (who had been visiting the property's caretaker) in his car in the driveway. Watson was first to enter the house, where he found Frykowski asleep on the sofa and told him, "I'm the devil, and I'm here to do the devil's business." Sebring was shot and stabbed to death by Watson, before Frykowski was stabbed fifty-one times by Watson on the front lawn. Folger tried to escape, but Krenwinkel and Watson grabbed her and delivered twenty-eight fatal stab wounds.

Tate begged to save her unborn child's life but was stabbed to death by Atkins and Watson. Outside the house, Kasabian was the lookout and recalled hearing "horrifying sounds." As they were leaving, Atkins wrote "PIG" on the front door in Tate's blood, following Manson's order to "leave something witchy, a sign to let the world know you were there."

The next night, Manson accompanied these four followers, as well as Leslie van Houten and Steve "Clem" Grogan, to commit more murders in the Los Feliz neighborhood of Los Angeles. Manson randomly chose the home of grocery store executive Leno LaBianca and his wife Rosemary, ordering that the couple be murdered. Watson stabbed Leno to death, then Krenwinkel and van Houten killed Rosemary in her bedroom. Once more they left a gruesome calling card; van Houten carved "War" into Leno's chest with a fork and Krenwinkel wrote "Rise," "Death to Pigs," and "Helter Skelter" in his blood on the refrigerator.

Manson was a white supremacist who wanted to spark a race war; leaving these slogans was his way of suggesting all seven murders had been committed by Black Americans or the Black Panthers. In his warped, drug-addled mind, Manson believed the Beatles song "Helter Skelter," about a fairground ride, predicted a forthcoming race war. When this began, he planned to go underground before coming out to rule the Black population.

At the trial, female followers carved Xs into their foreheads to replicate Manson's.

BACK BEHIND BARS

In December 1969, Manson, Watson, Atkins, Krenwinkel, and van Houten were arrested. When their trial began in July 1970, Kasabian became the prosecution's principal witness against them in return for complete immunity. The trial became a circus for Manson's other followers who attended the courtroom each day, declaring their love for him and even detonating a small bomb to disrupt proceedings. "This was all completely scripted by Charlie," Krenwinkel said.

On January 25, 1971, Atkins, Manson, Krenwinkel, and van Houten were found guilty of first-degree murder and given the death penalty, but in 1972, the California Supreme Court ruled this was unconstitutional and all their sentences were reduced to life in prison. In October, Watson was found guilty and sentenced to death, also later reduced to life in prison.

CASE NOTES: ASSASSINATION ATTEMPT

Manson remained in prison until his death at the age of 83 in November 2017, but some followers remained active, most notably when they attempted to assassinate President Gerald Ford. On September 5, 1975, Ford was visiting the California Governor Jerry Brown in Sacramento when he was approached by a member of the Manson Family, 26-year-old Lynette "Squeaky" Fromme, in the grounds of the California state capitol.

Fromme had a Colt .45 pistol in a leg holster, drew it, and pointed it at the president's waist. There was no round in the gun's chamber and so there was no shot, just the sound of a click and Fromme saying, "It wouldn't go off." She later said she had not loaded the gun as she did not want to kill the president. Fromme was disarmed and restrained by Secret Service agent Larry Buendorf, and Ford continued to his meeting. Fromme was tried and spent the next thirty-four years in prison before being released in August 2009.

AUM

SHINRIKYO

LOCATION: .... JAPAN

YEARS ACTIVE: .... 1987-PRESENT DAY

FOUNDER: .... SHOKO ASAHARA

On a spring morning in 1995, hundreds of people set off on the Tokyo subway, just like the start of any other day. What happened next sent shockwaves around the world. Five cars on three subway lines had been infiltrated with the liquid nerve agent sarin, killing thirteen people and affecting thousands, the worst domestic terrorist attack ever carried out on Japanese soil. Who would perpetrate such an awful crime and why? Suspicion soon fell on a seemingly obscure religious group. Its name was Aum Shinrikyo.

In March 1955, in the city of Yatsushiro in southeast Japan, Shoko Asahara was born into an impoverished family. Suffering with a congenital glaucoma, Asahara was partially blind and attended a specialist school. He was reportedly a bad student, bullying his classmates and stealing their money, but having graduated in 1977, he turned to the more enlightened career option of acupuncture and traditional Chinese medicine.

Shoko Asahara, pictured here in Moscow in 1994, enjoyed a global following.

Having moved to Tokyo, he began to study astrology, but in 1982, Asahara had his first notable run-in with the police when he was caught and fined for violating drug laws and practicing pharmacy without a license. It was around this time that Asahara turned to religion. His first beliefs stemmed from Agon Shū, a Japanese Buddhist sect that brought three modes of the religion—Northern Buddhism (Mahayana), Southern Buddhism (Theravada/Hinayana), and Vajrayana—together. From his small, one-bedroomed apartment in the city, Asahara began conducting yoga sessions, and in time he claimed to have attained Nirvana. Having released images of himself seemingly levitating, he began to procure followers who would attend his talks on his own acquisition of psychic powers.

By 1987, Asahara had called his growing group Aum Shinrikyo (Supreme Truth). Taking elements from Buddhism, Hinduism, and Christianity, Asahara saw his number of members swell to 1,300. With growing interest, he began to preach regularly, claiming to be Buddha, a reincarnation of Shiva (the Hindu god of destroying evil), and the Christ Messiah (messenger of God). His aim, he told his members, was to build the mythical state of Shambhala, a utopian kingdom. He wrote books on the subject and in time created communities where he indoctrinated both male monks and female nuns who lived isolated lives, while promising them that, in time, they could also become Buddhas.

A DANGEROUS RISE

In 1989, Aum Shinrikyo earned official status as a religious group and quickly saw its numbers and bank balance rise. Popular with students at elite universities, who were drawn to the group and its leader's promise of enlightened, less pressurized lives, the group's membership grew from 4,000 in 1988 to 10,000 in 1992, and then peaked at a reported 60,000 worldwide by 1995.

While the group and Asahara urged followers to reject materialism, large financial donations were made and former members have spoken about strange financial gains made by Aum Shinrikyo, including the sale of locks of Asahara's hair and his bathwater. One former member admitted to spending almost $10,000 on a vial of the leader's blood, which he drank as part of an initiation. The group published books and magazines, and used Japanese animation and large advertisement campaigns to articulate their message. They claimed to offer members cures for any physical ailments, and tips for a healthier lifestyle and for improving intelligence and positivity. Seen as new

Members of the doomsday cult parade on the streets of Tokyo in 1990, wearing masks depicting the face of their guru.

and exciting, while moving away from traditional, seemingly old-fashioned modes of religion, Aum Shinrikyo became one of Japan's fastest-growing religious entities.

In time, however, rumors of a murkier nature began to materialize. Talk of heavy drug use, shock therapy, and the extortion of donations became louder, and allegations of violence and even murder became rife. One member who wanted to leave disappeared, and it was said that he had been killed by the group's hierarchy.

In 1989, anti-cult lawyer Tsutsumi Sakamoto had started a class-action lawsuit against Aum Shinrikyo, which he hoped would see them go bankrupt. In November of that year, the lawyer, his wife, and their infant son went missing from their home near Tokyo. Police could not find the bodies, and while Sakamoto's colleagues publicly aired their suspicions of the group, no legal action could be taken.

MASS MURDER

By the early 1990s, the cult and its leader had become increasingly aggressive, their message more and more deadly. Convinced that the world was soon to end, Asahara took from the Christian Bible, preaching that "Armageddon" was coming and that only members of his group would survive an impending World War III.

The group's numbers had grown internationally, but when Asahara and twenty-three of his group tried but failed to gain political traction in elections in 1990, they blamed the Freemasons and Jews for their failure and began to turn their focus from being a religious entity to a militarized one.

Asahara started to focus on the impending war with the USA. The group built strongholds in the Japanese countryside that included small factories, in which scientists (300 were now recruited) began to create a chemical stockpile. In 1992, a medical mission was sent to Zaire in Africa under the ruse that it was helping to combat the Ebola outbreak, but in reality those scientists were there to obtain and harbor the disease. They were unsuccessful, but in 1993, the group began to secretly manufacture the nerve agent sarin. Asahara ordered that it should be tested at a sheep farm in Western Australia, where it killed twenty-nine animals. It was now time to use it at home.

Aum Shinrikyo's aim was to overturn the government and assassinate judicial figures who were against them. In June 1994, a chemical attack on the city of Matsumoto, near the home of three opposing judges, killed eight people. The police had no evidence to charge Asahara or any of the cult, but at the start of 1995, three murders of members who were thought to be spies or opposed to the hierarchy put Asahara under suspicion. Having been tipped off that the police were planning raids on his premises, Asahara hoped to divert their attention and ordered the attack on the Tokyo subway.

On the morning of March 20, 1995, thirteen people were killed, fifty-four were seriously injured, and a reported 6,000 members of the public were affected when bags of sarin on five different trains leaked their poison. An outraged nation demanded justice. The hunt was on for Asahara and his cult.

THE AFTERMATH

Now on the run, the group continued its murderous campaign, unsuccessfully attempting to release hydrogen cyanide in several train stations. The police were under huge pressure to make arrests and while members were charged with other crimes, it was not until May 16 that Asahara was found hiding within the wall of a building. Along with several other cult members, he was charged with the subway attacks.

Victims of the sarin attack on the Tokyo subway receive medical attention.

By now, due to raids on many of their factories, the scale of the group's activities became clear. Explosives, chemical weapons, a Russian military helicopter, and enough stockpiles of sarin to kill 4 million people were all found. Once charged, members admitted to many murders, including that of the lawyer Tsutsumi Sakamoto and his family. After a huge trial, Asahara was found guilty and sentenced to death, alongside twelve other members. The hunt continued for others responsible and as late as 2012 another perpetrator, Katsuya Takahashi, was caught and sentenced to life in prison for his part in the attack.

Asahara was executed in 2018, and Aum Shinrikyo is still classified as a terrorist group by US authorities, believed to be active underground. A former spokesman for the group, Fumihiro Joyu, started a splinter group called Hikari No Wah (Circle of Rainbow Light) and has distanced himself from the former cult and its murderous past.

CASE NOTES: SARIN

The deadly agent used by Aum Shinrikyo in the Tokyo attack was first discovered in 1938 by German scientists, but fearing similar retaliation, Adolf Hitler refused to use it in World War II. In 1950, NATO nations and the Soviets adopted it as a chemical weapon.

In 1988, five thousand Kurds were killed by a sarin attack by Iraqi forces, and it has been used with deadly effect during the recent Syrian War. The agent has no odor but attacks the nervous system, causing extreme physical reactions, from running eyes and nose to vomiting and the emptying of bowels and the bladder. If exposure is great enough these can progress to convulsions, paralysis, and death within one to ten minutes. However, if a victim survives an attack, antidotes are available and there are not necessarily any long-term effects.

ORDER OF THE SOLAR TEMPLE

LOCATION:............... SWITZERLAND AND CANADA

YEARS ACTIVE:....................................... 1984-97

FOUNDERS:............................. LUC JOURET AND
JOSEPH DI MAMBRO

The Order was a mystical and elitist group, guided by New Age
teachings, that claimed to be the heirs of the medieval Knights
Templar, the Christian warriors who guarded the Holy Grail. A
secret society influenced by the occult, members dressed in white
robes and hoods, meeting in hidden underground chapels, before
tragedy struck in a series of coordinated mass death events.

Di Mambro with his wife, Jocelyne, and daughter, Emmanuelle, who he claimed was the Messiah.

The cult was formed by Luc Jouret and Joseph Di Mambro in Geneva, Switzerland, in 1984. Jouret had been born in Congo to Belgian parents in 1947. After studying in Brussels and serving as a paratrooper in the Belgian Army, he qualified to become a homeopathic physician in France. He practiced homeopathy in Annemasse, near the Swiss border, and traveled around giving lectures on holistic health and the paranormal, including to the Golden Way Foundation, a New Age group inspired by the Knights Templar, in Geneva, which was run by Di Mambro.

The pair formed a bond and founded their own secret organization, the Order of the Solar Temple. The charismatic Jouret became the public face of the cult and spread its message worldwide, particularly in Europe and Canada. The Montreal Crown prosecutor Jean-Claude Boyer told The Canadian Press news agency in 1994 that Jouret looked like a "gentleman," and recruited people who "looked like businessmen."

Meanwhile Di Mambro had a more day-to-day presence and helped to run the Order. Born in 1924, the Frenchman had already been involved with the Rosicrucian group AMORC, which followed Christian mysticism, trained as a spiritualist medium, and spent time in prison for minor fraud. He has been described as "a confidence trickster who made a successful career masquerading as a psychologist."

THE GROWTH OF THE ORDER

The Order moved to Zurich, opening regional lodges across the country and in Canada, with around a thousand members at its peak. Jouret and Di Mambro offered expensive personal spiritual courses informed by occult disciplines and New Ages principles, which appealed to the wealthy and upper-middle classes who wanted something radical.

The pair opened lodges with chapels, where members would congregate wearing long, white robes adorned with red crosses, and use private rituals, secret codes, and symbols. New members would have to undergo initiation ceremonies and promise not to reveal what happened. The Order had a hierarchy, and its members were encouraged to work their way through the different levels, to reach its inner sanctum.

"We were disengaged and disconnected from everything," former member Herman Delorme has said. "Nothing else mattered. All your life was at the temple. It flatters your ego to be part of a group that designs itself as an elite, we were the chosen ones."

"We were completely taken over by Di Mambro's personality, like a child who loves his father," said another former member, Thierry Huguenin. Di Mambro would tell his followers he could show them the ghosts of legends and religious artifacts from the past, including the blood of Christ, the Ark of the Covenant, the Holy Grail, and Excalibur, which proved just how special they all were. In reality Di Mambro used illusions created by lighting tricks and holograms. When any members went to Di Mambro with their doubts about what they were seeing, he instead convinced them there were reincarnations of great saints. Meanwhile, Jouret, who came to believe he was the third reincarnation of Jesus Christ, would ask the Order's female members to have sex with him so he could gain some "spiritual strength."

"WHAT WE'LL DO WILL BE MORE SPECTACULAR"

By the start of the 1990s, the Order started to experience problems: some disillusioned members left and spoke out about their doubts. This alerted the authorities who harbored fears they could even be a terrorist threat. Jouret was arrested for attempting to buy guns in Quebec.

It is believed that in the fall of 1994, Jouret and Di Mambro began to plot their gruesome exit. A tape was later found in which they could be heard talking. Di Mambro said, "People have beaten us to the punch, you know." Jouret replied, "Well, yeah. Waco beat us to the punch." Di Mambro then declared, "In my opinion, we should have gone six months before them . . . what we'll do will be even more spectacular."

On September 30, 1994, Antonio Dutoit, his wife Nicky Robinson Dutoit, and their three-month-old son Emmanuel were stabbed to death with wooden stakes at the Order's center in Morin Heights, Quebec. It is believed Di Mambro had ordered their murders as he thought the baby was the Antichrist and had been born to thwart his aims. Their bodies were found in a burning chalet four days later, on October 4, with a pair of Swiss citizens also found dead in a nearby chalet.

The pair's plans were carried out the next day, October 5, with the mass deaths that saw a total of forty-eight members in the Swiss villages of Cheiry

Twenty-three followers of the Order were found dead inside this Swiss farmhouse in October 1995.

and Salvan either commit suicide or be murdered by the Order. Emergency services were called to a fire at a farmhouse in Cheiry. Fire crews battled with the flames but were unable to save most of the house before entering the charred wreckage. Inside they found the body of the farm's owner, 73-year-old Alberto Giacobino, who had a plastic bag over his head and had been shot. On further investigation, they found a hidden underground chamber, a garage converted into a chapel lined with mirrors. Here they found twenty-two more bodies wearing ceremonial robes lying in a circle with their feet together, plastic bags over their heads. Most of the bodies had gunshot wounds, some had been drugged, and according to *The Toronto Sun*, among the dead were a local mayor, a newspaper reporter, and a civil servant.

"It was frightful to enter a place like that and find so many dead," Swiss police spokesman Beat Karten told reporters. "It's atrocious. Atrocious."

An hour later, 60 miles (95 kilometers) south in Salvan, more fire crews were called out to two burning chalets where they found twenty-five more bodies, including eight children, who had been shot, poisoned, or suffocated. In the space of a single day, fifty-three bodies, all members of the Order of the Solar Temple, were found across two continents.

It is believed Jouret and Di Mambro had enjoyed a "last supper" with other leading figures in the Order before commencing with the mass death. It is thought some members committed suicide, while others were shot or forced to take poison. Jouret and Di Mambro were found dead in Salvan. The Order sent four letters to the Swiss and French media claiming their members were escaping the "oppression of this world," which they believed would end soon. They had decided to leave their earthly bodies to travel to the star Sirius to enjoy a new life.

"They saw themselves as superior human beings whose survival was needed to 'relaunch' the human race after a cataclysm they saw coming because of the deterioration in world affairs," Boyer told The Canadian Press.

No one has been held responsible for these mass deaths. In the spring of 2001, one of the few surviving leaders of the Order, Michel Tabachnik, a celebrated Swiss conductor who had known Di Mambro since the 1970s, was put on trial in Grenoble, France, but acquitted. The prosecution appealed, but Tabachnik was once again cleared in December 2006.

Five members of
the Order killed
themselves in this
house in Saint-
Casimir, Quebec,
in March 1997.

CASE NOTES: COPYCAT MASS DEATHS

Despite the deaths of Di Mambro and Jouret, the Order continued in a diminished form and the following year its members took part in another mass death event. On December 23, 1995, sixteen bodies were found at a retreat at Vercors, in the mountains of southeastern France.

The deaths had taken place about a week earlier, and the bodies of cult members who had been shot or burned were found laid out in a star formation. One was Edith Bonlieu, the Olympic skier who had competed at the 1956 Winter Games.

In March 1997, five more members of the Order were found dead in a house in Saint-Casimir, Quebec, with three teenage children found drugged in a nearby shed, their parents having taken their own lives.

MOVEMENT FOR THE RESTORATION OF THE TEN COMMANDMENTS OF GOD

LOCATION:.. UGANDA

YEARS ACTIVE:................................... 1989-2000

FOUNDER:................................... PAULO KASHAKU

It began with religious visions: apparitions of one man's late daughter, comforting him in his grief. Then more apparitions, this time of the Virgin Mary, and more messages, straight from God. Soon the group increased in size, spreading its word. That word became apocalyptic, and as a new millennium approached, the lives of the cult's members became endangered. Then tragedy struck. Was this organized suicide or mass murder?

In 1960, a man from Uganda called Paulo Kashaku saw an apparition. There in front of him was his deceased daughter, and she began to talk. She told him that, in time, further visions from heaven would come to him. Twenty-eight years later, Kashaku told his family that at last those heavenly visions had appeared to him. St. Joseph, Jesus, and the Virgin Mary had come before him, and the family took it as a sign to dedicate their lives to the latter.

Kashaku owned land and he set about using it, building upon it to recruit fellow believers. One of his daughters, Credonia Mwerinde, was fully behind the new religious sect and along with her daughter, she obeyed her father's orders to take the word of the Blessed Mary around Uganda. In June 1989, Mwerinde, her daughter, and another follower of her father met with Joseph Kibwetere, a man well known in the country for his fervent Roman Catholic beliefs, his pious ways, and his dedication to prayer. He had opened a Catholic school; he had both money and land, and also claimed to have been visited by the Virgin Mary.

Kibwetere took the women's visit to him as a sign that he should join the group. Much to his own family's concern, he used the land he owned to build more schools teaching the group's beliefs, and even invited Mwerinde and others to live with them. They were joined by nuns who would theologize over the leaders' messages, and priests who had been defrocked by the Catholic Church. The Movement for the Restoration of the Ten Commandments of God (RTCG) had been formed.

THE CULT GROWS

In 1991, Kashaku died and was replaced as leader by Kibwetere. The following year, the growing cult moved to the village of Kanungu in the western district of Rukungini. There were almost a thousand members,

The Virgin Mary was said to have visited senior members of the religious group.

and while the community lived in seeming austerity, homes, churches, an office, and more schools were built. The group's message became increasingly reactionary, using the experiences of their visitations from Jesus and Mary. New followers—disenchanted by the country and its politicians—were attracted to their preaching and beliefs.

When Father Dominic Kataribaabo, an American-educated priest, became one of its leaders in 1992, the group had real credibility and numbers began to swell further. Many other priests joined but most were excommunicated as the Roman Catholic Church wanted to distance themselves from what was becoming an ever more radicalized and archconservative movement.

EMERGENCE OF EVIL

In 1996, with membership thriving, Dr. Kataribaabo wrote and edited a new edition of the group's manifesto. Entitled *A Timely Message from Heaven: The End of Present Times*, it reiterated the group's message that the Bible's Ten Commandments had been too long discarded by the modern world, but it also had more sinister content.

"All of you living on the Planet, listen to what I'm going to say: When the year 2000 is completed, the year that will follow will not be year 2001. The year that will follow shall be called Year One in a generation that will follow the present generation; the generation that will follow will have few or many people depending on who will repent. The Lord told me that hurricanes of fire would rain forth from heaven and spread over all those who would not have repented."

Members had long been subject to strict rules. Sex, even between married couples, was severely frowned upon and discouraged. Communication itself was limited to a sign language, as silence was held sacred. The Roman Catholic Church continued to distance itself, angered by the group's leaders' (heretic) claims that they had spoken to God himself.

It wasn't only members who were harshly treated. Juvenal Rugambwa, who claimed to be Kibwetere's son, later told the *New York Times* that his father, hitherto a loving and gentle man, had become increasingly aggressive as the group grew. "We grew up in a lovely home, a lovely family, until he brought those people home," he said. "When the people came here they started mistreating us, the family members, the children, and the mother, saying the Virgin Mary had told them to do things, to keep us without food and to punish us."

While Rugambwa and much of Kibwetere's natural family managed to leave the group, its membership grew. It is estimated that at its peak numbers were as high as 5,000, and as their riches grew, further homes, offices, and a school were built. In 1998, the Ugandan government, fully aware and skeptical of the leaders, shut down the school, citing unsanitary conditions, possible child labor, and even suspected kidnapping. However, such was the power of the group that any efforts to fully shut it down were futile, and soon the school was reopened.

In 1999, a state-owned Ugandan newspaper called *New Vision* ran an interview with a teenage member of the movement. He said, "The world ends next year. There is no time to waste. Some of our leaders talk directly to God. Any minute from now, when the end comes, every believer who will be at an as yet undisclosed spot will be saved."

A FATEFUL DAY

With the prophesied doomsday of January 1, 2000, looming, the movement's actions became increasingly frantic. Members sold possessions and cattle, sins were confessed in the hope of redemption, past members returned, and slowly all labor in the fields ceased. The day came and went without incident. Questions needed to be answered.

Some members rebelled, demanding their money back, but the leaders refused. Instead they backtracked and a new date of March 17 was set. When that day arrived, a big party was arranged at Kanungu, and it was during those "festivities" that an explosion was heard from nearby villages. Up to 530 members had arrived for the party, but when the authorities came to investigate the explosion, they discovered that the windows and doors of the church had been boarded up, locking in all the members, who consequently perished in a fire.

At first, investigators presumed that this was a religious sect's organized mass suicide, but they discovered that the leaders had killed another 395 members in attacks at compounds across Uganda three weeks prior to the fire at Kanungu.

None of the five principal leaders (Joseph Kibwetere, Joseph Kasapurari, John Kamagara, Dominic Kataribaabo, and Credonia Mwerinde) were formally identified as dead in the fire, and the Ugandan President, Yoweri Museveni, condemned them and the event as a "mass murder by these priests for monetary gain." An international warrant for the arrest of the leaders was issued but none have ever been found and many believe that they did, in fact, take their own lives in the fire. Days before the explosion, Kibwetere's family received a package containing books and documents, and a request to continue the movement's message. They never did, and while some still believe that the leaders escaped with the movement's riches, nothing has ever been proved.

The charred remains of dozens of the hundreds of victims killed by the cult's leaders.

Uganda was deeply troubled throughout the 1970s and '80s, with warfare and violence a constant threat.

CASE NOTES: A TROUBLED NATION

Under the brutal dictatorship of Idi Amin, Uganda and its people had suffered throughout the 1970s. Civil war had been followed by the AIDS epidemic in the 1980s, and with the Catholic Church unable to sustain any mass support due to its own scandals and corruption in the country, many of the population looked elsewhere for their spiritual guidance.

By the late 1980s, hundreds of religious sects preyed on the void left by politicians and the Catholic Church, and with often apocalyptic messages, they sustained great support. Paul Ikazire was a leading member within the RTCG, and despite having left long before the murders, he explained their early motives to *The New York Times*. "We joined the movement as a protest against the Catholic Church. We had good intentions. The church was backsliding, the priests were covered in scandals, and the AIDS scourge was taking its toll on the faithful. The world seemed poised to end."

2

NUDISM, ABUSE, AND SEXUAL EXPLOITATION

Sex, or a horribly warped version
of it, is at the heart of many
dangerous cults. We take a look
at seven of them, including
the Ant Hill Kids, whose leader
Roch Thériault convinced nine
of his female followers to let
him impregnate them to produce
twenty-six children, and the Sarah
Lawrence cult, where a student's
father moved into her dorm and
co-opted her housemates into a
sex cult, even sending one student
into prostitution.

THE
FREEDOMITES

LOCATION:............................ KRESTOVA, CANADA

YEARS ACTIVE:.................... 1902-PRESENT DAY

FOUNDER:.. UNKNOWN

They came from a faraway land, in search of a better life. What began
as simple prayer meetings with hymns about their beliefs ended in
isolation, anarchic protest, and eventually terrorism, murder, and
imprisonment. When the Freedomites (aka Sons of Freedom) came
to Canada at the start of the twentieth century, the new life they hoped
for fell apart, and the division between their beliefs and those of
mainstream society grew into a turbulent conflict.

God's People rejected many of the Russian Orthodox Church's beliefs and icons.

A religious group in Imperial Russia in the seventeenth and eighteenth centuries went by the name of "God's People." While the Russian Orthodox Church was all-powerful in the country, this was a vocal group who rejected their rituals, their icons, their beliefs, and the idea that the Bible is the supreme source of divine revelation.

Russian political and church leaders were unsurprisingly perturbed. In 1734, an edict was issued against the movement and any similar group that rejected their pious symbols. There began a decades-long persecution of the group, and as the years passed, archbishops denounced them as heretics. By the beginning of the nineteenth century, the group had renamed themselves the Doukhobors, but with the new organization came further controversial ideologies, including pacifism. While they opposed any military action, the imperialistic Tsar (Alexander I), alongside the church, took further measures to weaken and oppress them, according to the group's sympathizers.

In 1826, the Tsar strongly encouraged the migration of religious minorities to regions in what is today southern Ukraine. By moving the Doukhobors from the country's heartlands, the Tsar and his religious leaders hoped to rid the nation of such "anti-Russian" ideology. It was another example of discrimination and began years of both forced and voluntarily migration.

When Tsar Nicholas I succeeded Alexander, he issued decrees stipulating that all eligible members of "dissenting religious groups" be conscripted into the military where they would serve in the Caucasus. Between 1841 and 1845, 5,000 Doukhobors were resettled in Georgia, and as the century progressed, leaders were exiled to Siberia, and their place in Tsarist Russia became increasingly problematic.

What set the Doukhobors apart was their resistance to perceived Russian regulations and laws, as well as orthodox religion. The registration of marriages and births was opposed, and so too was the contribution of grains and crops to forced state emergency funds. When Tsar Nicholas II came to power in 1894, they refused to swear allegiance, and further rebellion led to their members being beaten by state Cossacks (a semi-military group) and many that fled their homes died of starvation.

It was then, in the final years of the nineteenth century, that the Tsar and his government agreed that the Doukhobors could leave the country (at their own expense), and when land was granted to them by the Canadian government, it was decided that this was to be their new home. In 1902, with no designated Doukhobor leader (they were still exiled in Serbia), an initially small faction broke from the Doukhobors. In time they were a fully independent group that went by the name of the Freedomites.

BELIEFS AND PUBLIC PROTESTS

While life in Canada was a far cry from the oppressive nature of Tsarist Russia, locals were just as mistrustful of the Doukhobors and the new Freedomites. The Freedomites' meetings were similar to those conducted in Russia. Protestant in nature, they took place in simple buildings, the benches were wooden, and the hymns and prayers sung and spoken in their mother tongue. They spoke of matters of community, the desire for peaceful, rural lives, and the continued rejection of governmental regulations.

It was a letter written by a Doukhobor leader called Peter V. Verigin in 1896 that was scrutinized by the Freedomites and shaped their deep-rooted beliefs in the education (or lack of it) of their children. In the letter, Verigin wrote, "Our society's age-old views of education are reprehensible and we have very few educated people among us. The few, if any, are self-taught.

An abandoned Doukhobor prayerhouse sits in the landscape of Saskatchewan, Canada.

We maintain that education destroys the inclination to greet people, also schools corrupt the morals of children, and thirdly all things through which education is actualized are obtained through great hardships, therefore, to participate in the subjugation of people in any form must be avoided."

When around 3,000 Freedomites settled in the Saskatchewan region of the country, they abided by these teachings and began to refuse their children entry to the school. The Canadian government stepped in and many of the parents were charged for the offence. Soon, Freedomite members were protesting on the streets and outside the prisons in which others were held. These public protests received huge national interest, with many of the members choosing to be nude, not only to attract more attention but to underline their core belief that the wearing of clothes was immoral and that the skin that God had made was more perfect than any man-made cloth.

PROTESTS TURN TO VIOLENCE

At first, by way of protest, the Freedomites would burn their possessions, including cash, but from the early 1920s up to the 1960s, protests turned to terrorism as the use of explosives (first used in 1923) and arson saw the destruction (often done in the nude) of schools, Doukhobor neighbors' properties, and even their own buildings. In 1924, a train was blown up. On board was Peter Verigin, no longer in exile, and said to have been assassinated due his distancing from the group.

With the economic crisis in the 1930s, followed by World War II, the group's numbers increased and their resolve grew. Nude parades persisted into the post-war years as did the bombings and arson attacks. It is said that up to a dozen people died from the violent protests, and in 1962, several Freedomites were imprisoned on terrorist charges. While violent acts became less common, relatives of the jailed men and women set out on what they called the Long March, a 400-mile (640-kilometer) walk from Krestova to Vancouver and on to the Mountain Institution in Agassiz, originally opened as a prison for Freedomites, where they remained in situ for months in support of their interned friends and relatives.

Canada's Mounted Police were enlisted to help enforce Operation Snatch.

OPERATION SNATCH

Between 1953 and 1959, up to 200 children of members of the Freedomites were taken by the Canadian government to be placed in care. It was called Operation Snatch and while carried out under the guise of "educational welfare," the children were placed in an overcrowded, prison-like institution in British Columbia. Parents were only permitted to visit from behind a fence, and those whose children were released were made to swear an oath that they would send them to a Canadian school. In 1959 they were all released, but over the years there have been many accounts of widespread physical and sexual abuse. Demands for a government apology have yet to be answered, but in 2004, Geoff Plant, a member of the British Columbia Legislative Assembly, delivered a "Statement of Regret." Today there are thought to be around 30,000 Doukhobors in Canada, around 2,500 of those being descendants of the Freedomites. Many of them continue to campaign for an apology.

CASE NOTES: FLORENCE (FANNY) STORGOFF

One of the Freedomites' most infamous leaders was a woman called Fanny Storgoff. Storgoff had come to Canada from Russia, aged three. She had moved to California aged 15 but returned to Vancouver to be married before settling in Krestova with her husband. Krestova had become the Freedomite capital and at the height of the protests, she served time for both public nudity and arson.

In 1962, as leader, Storgoff led a thousand Freedomites on the Long March, at the end of which they camped at the Mountain Institution and protested for the release of their relatives. Storgoff died from cancer in 1964, aged 56. An impressive woman, even a Mounted Police officer who accompanied the group on the march remarked that, "If Fanny had decided to run a hospital or a department store, or almost anything, she would have been a success. She might have been a great woman if the circumstances had been different."

THE
SULLIVANIANS

LOCATION:........................NEW YORK CITY, USA

YEARS ACTIVE:.....................................1957-91

FOUNDER:..............................SAUL B. NEWTON

In an affluent, sought-after area of Manhattan, intellectuals, artists, lawyers, doctors, and writers gathered. They didn't like the term "cult," but to the outside world, that's exactly what it was. The group and its leader were anticonformist, anti-establishment, and antimonogamy. Their methods raised eyebrows, even during the enlightened 1960s and 1970s, and they became increasingly sinister. Families were split apart; children were abandoned. This was the Sullivanians.

Saul B. Newton (original family name Cohen) was born in New Brunswick, Canada, in 1906. Having attended the University of Wisconsin, he moved on to study in Chicago. There, Newton associated with radicals, becoming a communist, antifascist unionist. In the 1930s, Newton traveled to Spain, where he fought with like-minded North Americans in the Spanish Civil War, and then with the US army in World War II.

The cult owned several properties in affluent areas of Manhattan.

Highly politicized, Newton turned his attentions to psychotherapy after the war and by 1957, he and his first wife, Dr. Jane Pearce, had founded the Sullivan Institute for Research in Psychoanalysis. Based in New York, the institute took its name from Harry Stack Sullivan, a cofounder of the William Alanson White Institute, where they both worked.

Sullivan, through his stringent studies of therapists such as Sigmund Freud and Adolf Meyer, sought to understand an individual based upon the network of relationships that they experience. Throughout the 1960s, the couple's group sessions initially attracted a small and informal following. This was a decade of "free love," and Newton's beliefs that it was the traditional nuclear family that was to blame for failing mental health resonated with his followers. He also began to advocate non-monogamous relationships, and as the 1960s became the 1970s, the therapy center and the group began to expand.

By the mid-1970s, the group's numbers had swelled to over 200. A subsidiary of the institute they had formed was a theater company called the Fourth Wall Repertory Company, which was based in the East Village. The group expanded to provide theatrical productions, therapy sessions, and a polyamorous commune.

In three buildings on the Upper West Side of Manhattan, at one point up to 500 members lived "together," with Newton (he had remarried and would have six wives in total) continuing to teach Marxist and Communist theories through his brand of psychotherapy, while he demanded polygamy with increasing rigidity. With the theater company and its many productions thriving, and its growing membership throughout the 1970s and into the 1980s, the Sullivanians (as they had become known) was by now a wealthy and successful organization.

Members, usually left-wing professionals, enjoyed the post-1960s' promise of revolution. Artists such as the writer Richard Price were reportedly involved, as was Jackson Pollock and the Grammy-award winning singer, Judy Collins. From the outside and perhaps to new members, it seemed to be a close-knit social gathering. But, within, things were far from relaxed, and soon the outside world would know it.

THE COURT CASE

By the end of the 1980s, the group's numbers had dwindled, but it was a custody case between one former member and his estranged wife in New York that finally lifted the lid on Newton and the Sullivanian's darker practices within the cult.

In the summer of 1988, Paul Sprecher, a former member of the group, sought custody of his five-year-old son from his wife (still a Sullivanian), Julia Agee. Sprecher had joined in 1974, attracted to the group's relaxed and social attitude to life. "It was this incredibly neat experience for a newcomer in New York City," he said. "Suddenly I had a social life. There were women who wanted to date me. We spent the summer in Amagansett. It was very loose in those days, just people hanging out in apartments."

However, in time Sprecher had concerns about the lifestyle the group advocated, and about the lack of boundaries within therapy sessions. He left in 1986. "The therapists did not regard therapeutic boundaries with any respect at all," Sprecher recalled. "Everyone slept with everyone."

In court, Sprecher argued that his ex-wife's lifestyle within the group made her unfit to continue as the mother of his son, and as the case continued,

Both Bray (left) and Sprecher (right) left the cult and took legal action against it.

details of what went on became increasingly sensational. "It's a sick, insane, revolting group that indulges in bizarre practices and maintains a manic, bunker mentality," said Sprecher's lawyer in court. "By every and any definition, it is a cult."

A SINISTER ORGANIZATION

The picture of the reality within Newton's group was clearly a strange one. Members living together in those Upper West Side blocks had to abide by strict rules. They lived in sex-segregated apartments, and engaging in "exclusive" relationships was forbidden, as was sex with anyone outside of the group.

Alarmingly, any children born within the group were quickly sent to boarding school, or given to "caretakers," where parents would be permitted to visit them for perhaps two hours a day. Other family relationships were also firmly discouraged. Within his therapy sessions, Newton advised the severing of members' previous family ties unless they were necessary for financial gain. Sprecher himself lost touch with his parents after only a few months of therapy.

Early members have since suggested that after Newton divorced his first wife, Dr. Pearce, things became progressively more erratic as his increasingly demanding nature came to the fore. Parties bordering on orgies were thrown regularly. "No one could say no [to sex]," said one member. There was financial exploitation too, one member being forced into "donating"

The nuclear plant on Three
Mile Island suffered a partial
meltdown in 1979, causing many
of the group to move to Florida.

$100,000, being told it would aid his "personal growth." In 1979, those demands became more erratic, and Newton's character more paranoid.

When the Three Mile Island nuclear plant suffered a partial meltdown, Newton, a vocal opponent of nuclear energy, moved members of the group to Florida, arguing that the accident was a preface for the destruction of New York. Three weeks later, and with the city still standing, Newton and the 250 members he took with him returned. Those who hadn't traveled were chastised, and shortly after, at a resort the group had acquired in the Catskills (Newton also had a property in Vermont), some members were sent to line the walls of a room with steel, so work could be done without interference from the CIA.

In the 1980s, his health deteriorating, Newton's erratic and paranoid behavior became more menacing, even violent. Those seen as being against him or wanting to leave were either intimidated, or in the case of Michael Cohen, attacked. In 1985, having made his intentions to leave the cult known, Cohen was followed to the Union Square subway station, where he was attacked by two Sullivanians who dangled him near the tracks and threatened to kill him.

THE END

As well as the much-publicized court case between Sprecher and Agee, another former member, Michael Bray, brought a similar action for custody of his twin daughters. With these cases, public opinion of Newton and his group continued to diminish. His violence and controlling ways, and the activities of the group, were now out in the open, and membership fell drastically. By the time Newton died in 1991, his cult had no successor to lead, and it disappeared completely.

While the cult's practices have been widely criticized and former members are mainly vocal in their disgust of the group they once belonged to, there are some who look back fondly on its existence. Eric Grunin, a member for twelve years, was asked in 2016 if the Sullivanians could exist today. "Of course it will happen again," he replied. "People want that. People need alternatives."

CASE NOTES: A FORCED "KIDNAPPING"

By the mid-1980s, Saul Newton and members of his group had become increasingly aggressive and despotic. In 1985, in retaliation against paint being thrown on the cult's building, a group led by Newton's son, Robbie, attacked another block, breaking toilets and TVs, slashing mattresses, and striking inhabitants with sticks.

A year later, a member called Marice Pappo had her baby girl taken away from her while she breastfed and handed over to the father and the "caretakers." Having managed to leave the group, Pappo felt she had to act to be reunited with her child. "I knew that if I didn't kidnap her, I would never see her again," she told a court. "What we went through has ruined our lives."

CHILDREN

OF GOD

LOCATION............................ USA AND WORLDWIDE

YEARS ACTIVE:..................... 1968-PRESENT DAY

FOUNDER:.. DAVID BERG

Evangelical preacher David Berg began by promising his followers
eternal happiness, but his religious sect became a dangerous sex ring
where children and women were routinely abused. Berg told cult
members they needed to prepare for the end of the world, the
"Endtime," which was coming in 1993. He declared that when
the end came, the only way to get to heaven was to abide by his rules.

In the summer of 1968, at a coffee shop in Huntington Beach,
California, Berg founded a group called "Teens for Christ" for
disaffected young people to learn about Christianity. It started with
fifty members but soon grew into "The Children of God," a hugely
controversial group, branded a cult by the authorities, with up to
10,000 members in 130 communities across 70 countries.

Berg offered to save
his followers' souls
through devotion to
Christ and the cult.

Born in 1919 in Oakland, California, Berg's parents were pastors who moved to Miami, Florida, to run a collection of churches. Berg would go on to become a minister himself in Valley Farm, Arizona, but was sacked after being accused of sexual misconduct. Berg went on the road, often with his mother, to work as a faith healer and preach his message of the benefits of a life devoted to Christ. Returning to California at the time of the Summer of Love and the growing counter-culture youth movement, he preached to the hippie generation about free love, finding happiness, and saving souls. After assembling his small group, Berg took them on the road around the USA to find new recruits. The movement soon developed into a collection of communes around the world.

To assert control over his followers Berg banished the concept of the family unit, insisting the group was one big family. Children were not allowed to attend school, but were educated instead within the commune. No one could work and all possessions had to be abandoned. "Everything was broken down so the parents didn't have control over the raising of the children. Parental authority was abdicated to the community," said Jeanette Solano, associate professor of religious studies at California State University, Fullerton.

The families of the Hollywood actors River and Joaquin Phoenix and Rose McGowan were members of the group, and for a time they were raised in these communes.

Berg convinced his followers that abiding by these rules was essential if they wanted salvation when the world came to an end. "I often spent my nights fantasizing about arriving in heaven after my death [in 1993]," former follower Flor Edwards said. "I would be given unearthly superpowers and a new heavenly body. I would never grow old . . . There would be lush gardens and tropical fields and we could eat freely from fruit trees. There would be no war and everlasting peace."

WIDESPREAD ABUSE

At the heart of Berg's philosophy was his belief that sex should be encouraged in all its forms, including incest, sex between adults and children, and sex between children. There should be no boundaries and his followers should freely express their sexuality. "God created boys and girls able to have children by 12 years old," he declared. "Now he is advocating child sex and child brides. Yes."

He promoted "sexual sharing" within his communes, allowing his followers to have sex with whoever and whenever they wanted. "I was convinced it was

A Children of God rally in 1971, the year that the cult's leader went into hiding.

like a duty," former follower Sylvia Padilla said. "Sometimes you were revolted, but if you were asked and you refused you were labeled selfish, unloving and that you didn't belong."

This created an environment where child abuse and sexual crimes were rampant. "It definitely wasn't a safe place to grow up, especially if you were a girl," former member Michael Young has said. "Close friends of mine growing up were abused and raped."

A 1974 report for the New York Attorney General detailed how a 14-year-old girl was raped when she refused to have sex with older members of the group and then placed in solitary confinement. Child rape and the ban of any contraception was used as a tool to "increase the tribe" and many unwanted pregnancies occurred across the communes. Berg encouraged his female members to recruit new males into the group by offering sex. The practice was called "flirty fishing" to suggest women could fish and hook men with their bodies.

THE SEXUAL PREDATOR

Berg himself was a notorious pedophile who preyed on children and used the group as his own personal sex ring. His daughter Deborah Davis alleged she had rejected a sexual advance from him. "My dad was an evil personality who was not hearing from God at all. I had to quit looking at him as my father but as the leader of a movement that was destroying people's lives."

One of Berg's granddaughters, Joyanne Treadwell Berg, claimed she was sexually abused by her grandfather. Another granddaughter, Merry Berg, claimed she was abused by members within the group and called her treatment "barbaric and cruel." In 2021, Serena Kelley spoke about the abuse she endured from Berg as a very young child while living in one of his communes in the Philippines during the 1980s. "It started when I was only a toddler," she told British newspaper *The Sun*. "I remember being groped by Berg, who I was encouraged to call 'Grandpa' when I was two, and learning to swim in his pool while an orgy took place. In 1986, when I was three, my mum led me to Berg's home where we were 'married.' An adult-sized heart-shaped ring with tape inside to make it smaller, was put on my tiny finger. My parents were thrilled, but I just saw him as a disgusting old man."

The leaders had to admit that they didn't know when Jesus would return.

REBRANDING A CULT

By 1993, Berg was finally investigated for the numerous allegations that had long surrounded him. Though he had been in hiding since 1971, he was wanted for questioning by the FBI in the USA, and in Argentina, France, Spain, Australia, Venezuela, and Peru. In 1994, he fled to Portugal, where he died at the age of 75.

"He was a deeply disturbed man with many demons," Edwards said. "He was a textbook narcissist who hid behind his teachings of God and his love. He was actually quite brilliant (in an intellectual sense) with a high IQ and very charismatic . . . He thought he was fulfilling God's mission, which is the most disturbing and dangerous part of it all. In his quest for power he hurt many people along the way. I think he in part died from guilt, one year after his predicted apocalypse."

In the wake of Berg's death, Karen Zerby, who was his personal secretary before becoming his wife, took control of the group and attempted to rebrand it. In 1978 it had already become The Family of Love, to sound less like a cult, then in 1982 became The Family. Since 2004, it has been known as The Family International. Zerby, who was known as Mama Maria, removed some of the rules. Now members could live outside the communes, send their children to school, have a normal job, and even marry partners who were not members of the group. By the start of 2009, Zerby and her new husband Steve Kelly had to acknowledge that the world was not going to end after all.

"The whole cult was built on the theory the Antichrist was coming so you didn't have to save for retirement," Angel Yamaguchi, a former member born into the group, told British newspaper *The Guardian*. "They've left a bunch of people that they've damaged struggling to try and cope and find out 'How do I move on?'"

The group still exists today, but despite its wish to forget its dark past, its reputation continues to be severely tarnished as a succession of survivors come forward with allegations of sexual abuse.

CASE NOTES: THE MO LETTERS

Berg communicated with his sprawling network through his "Mo Letters" (he sometimes used the name Moses David), a series of regular newsletters that contained his commandments of how he wanted his followers to live. They also included pornographic comic book drawings to convey his warped attitudes toward sex. During his reign spanning twenty-five years, he would distribute over 3,000 of these letters. Berg sought to control every aspect of his followers' lives this way, from the number of bathroom tissue sheets they should use, to who they should date, and where they should work and live.

"I used to read his writings and believe they had been inspired by God, and so I would obey them," Sylvia Padilla said.

ANT HILL

KIDS

LOCATION:................................ QUEBEC, CANADA

YEARS ACTIVE:.................................... 1977-89

FOUNDER:.............................. ROCH THÉRIAULT

Its name may sound innocent, but this small cult had a deranged leader who performed unimaginable horrors. During a hike in 1977, Roch Thériault claimed that he had heard and seen God, so he asked a group of friends to move to some remote woods to live with him on "holy land." The group became the Ant Hill Kids, which Thériault ruled over as a vicious tyrant for twelve years, subjecting his followers to constant abuse.

Roch Thériault was born in May 1947, in Saguenay, Quebec, to French–Canadian parents. He dropped out of school in the seventh grade at 13 years old and never managed to hold down a job for long. He read the Old Testament of the Bible, developed a doomsday obsession, and began to believe the world would soon end. He later became a member of the Seventh-Day Adventist Church.

By 1977, Thériault was living in Sainte-Maire, Quebec, and had come to believe he was a prophet and the people's savior. Despite his later crimes, his followers spoke about his overwhelming charisma and powerful motivational speaking, which he used to convince a small group of nine women, four men, and four children to establish a commune with him in woodland just outside the city. He told the group they could live a life free of sin and worry there, enjoy true equality and happiness, and prepare for the moment in February 1979 when he had been told by God that the world would end.

The cult built its base in remote woods at Saint-Jogues, on the Gaspé Peninsula.

After only a year, the cult hiked farther into the woods to an even more remote location at Saint-Jogues in the Gaspé Peninsula, which Thériault called "Eternal Mountain." There his followers built some cabins, and as they worked—while he watched and refused to help—he said they looked like worker ants on a hill and named them the Ant Hill Kids.

When the world did not end in February 1979 as predicted, Thériault told his followers it would still happen, and what they needed to do now was expand their group. To that end, Thériault convinced all nine female members to marry him and let him impregnate them, which would eventually produce a total of twenty-two children. As the commune grew in size, Thériault began to assert more control over it. The self-proclaimed prophet forbade his followers to have any contact with friends and family on the outside as it would dilute their relationship with him and with God. He then said they could only talk to one another with his permission. The women were all made to wear matching tunics.

TORTURE CAMP

Over time, Thériault began to reveal an even darker and more psychotic side to his nature, exacerbated by his heavy drinking. He used torture and violence to govern the commune and "purify" his followers. For any perceived transgression, he would beat his followers with a belt, a hammer, or the blunt side of an axe, and if a follower suggested they might want to leave, he would hang them from the ceiling and perform agonizing and degrading forms of torture on them.

Followers would be forced to prove their loyalty by committing various sadistic and dehumanizing acts, such as breaking their own legs with a sledgehammer, shooting each other in the shoulder, or cutting another follower's toes off with wire cutters. Thériault would also set up gladiatorial battles in which followers were forced to fight in a ring, sustaining broken bones and wounds, before he chose to stop the violence. His own children were not protected from the abuse, and if he believed they had misbehaved, punishments might include being held over hot ovens or nailed to trees while the other children threw rocks at them.

The followers sold baked goods, smoked fish, and maple syrup at the side of the road near the edge of the woods, and if they did not bring back enough money, Thériault would subject them to his torture regime. The abuse became so unrelenting that one of his wives left a two-month-old baby outside in a blizzard to freeze to death in the sub-zero temperatures, to escape the horrific life he would endure growing up at the commune.

THE CHILDREN ARE SAVED

In 1984, the group that now numbered around forty followers, with twenty adults and twenty children, moved to a new site in the woods of Burnt River, a hamlet in Ontario, just over 100 miles (160 kilometers) north of Toronto. They attracted some attention and soon the police and several agencies, including a representative from the Ministry of Community and Social Services, went to the commune to investigate.

An eerie sketch of Thériault was found hanging on the wall of his abandoned log cabin.

"As soon as the vehicles arrived, we could see all the people scatter . . . and the only person who emerged was Roch [Thériault]," said Bob Galipeau from the local Children's Aid Society. "They seemed healthy enough. We didn't have any immediate concerns . . . You need a reason to take those kids away. You can't just go on a gut feeling." But Galipeau also admitted his gut feeling was that something was not right about the commune, and though Thériault had been "cautiously polite," he felt he was hiding something, and the agencies began to investigate the cult's past and keep a closer watch on the activities of the group.

A year later, they had received a number of other reports that the children were at risk, and returned to remove a total of seventeen youngsters. "The mothers were given the chance to leave with their children, an opportunity most didn't take," said Galipeau. "Most of them decided not to because they were scared of him. They were scared he would haunt their dreams and come after them and kill them because they were brainwashed. Basically, he tortured everybody to get control over them."

AN ESCAPE REVEALS THE TRUTH

Incredibly, Thériault faced no further action. The children's removal did nothing to temper his violent behavior; he became even more extreme and deluded, believing he now had magical healing powers and could perform intricate medical surgeries.

After Thériault sadistically killed of one of his wives, Solange Boilard, in July 1989, another of his wives, Gabrielle Lavallée, attempted to escape.

Thériault used pliers to remove eight teeth from one of his wives who complained about toothache.

She had previously complained of toothache only for Thériault to remove eight of her teeth with pliers, among other forms of mutilation she had suffered at his hands. But Lavallée was quickly caught by Thériault, who took her back to the commune, removed one of her fingers, and amputated her arm.

The following month, on August 16, Lavallée made another attempt to escape, and this time was successful, hitchhiking her way to a hospital near Toronto. The truth was now finally revealed about the horrors occurring at the Ant Hill Kids' commune.

Thériault was found guilty of three counts of assault and one of unlawfully causing bodily harm for his attack on Lavallée, and sentenced to twelve years in prison. In 1993, he was also found guilty of the murder of Boilard, and had his sentence upgraded to life in prison. The cult faded away, but not before Thériault had fathered four more children with his followers on conjugal visits to him in prison.

CASE NOTES:
THE MURDER OF A MURDERER

On February 26, 2011, 63-year-old Thériault was murdered in his cell at Dorchester Penitentiary by his cellmate Matthew MacDonald, who stabbed him in the neck before telling a guard, "That piece of shit is down on the range. Here's the knife. I've sliced him up." MacDonald, who was already serving a sentence for murder, pleaded guilty to the second-degree murder of Thériault and was sentenced to life in prison.

ANGEL'S
─────────────────
LANDING
─────────────────

LOCATION:...................WICHITA, KANSAS, USA

YEARS ACTIVE:............................ 1996-2010

FOUNDER:...................................... LOU CASTRO

"Unexplained wealth." Those were the words of a local police officer who, his suspicions piqued, began to quietly investigate what he felt was a strange cult, living on a rural compound north of Wichita, in Kansas. Detective Ron Goodwyn of the Sedgwick County Sheriff's Office had noticed that the enigmatic leader, a man going by the name of Lou Castro, was living a lavish lifestyle that could not be vouched for by any significant employment. For nine years the detective watched the group, until in 2010, Castro was arrested and the horrific truth came out.

Lou Castro's Angel's
Landing group settled
in Wichita, Kansas,
in 2001.

When Lou Castro was arrested in 2010, the initial charge was ID fraud and theft. Under investigation, the authorities could find out very little about him. No employment records nor any other records of a man who less than a decade earlier had arrived in Wichita, looking to purchase property.

What was discovered was that Lou Castro was born Daniel Perez in November 1959. His early years were spent in Texas but there is no more information about his childhood or family members. As a young adult he worked as a mechanic in the navy. It has since emerged that he used aliases and was forced to change addresses more than once, following claims of pedophilia and molestation.

In time, Perez, now going under the name of Lou Castro, met a woman called Patricia Gomez. Castro was very charismatic and, having befriended Patricia, he would target young, vulnerable girls, convincing them that he possessed supernatural powers. In time, he became the head of the cult that he called Angel's Landing.

Cult members, some with children as young as eight, were told by Castro that he was possessed by three angels. One called Arthur, one called Daniel, and one named Amber. All three had different personalities, ranging from evil to friendly. He claimed that his powers included reincarnating the dead and controlling the weather. His most odious claim, however, was that should he not have sex with young girls, his powers would wane and he would die. Over time, the followers and their children believed his dangerous claims.

A GROWING GROUP

In the late 1990s, Castro, living in South Dakota, met a woman named Mona Griffith. She and her two teenage children moved in with him, while Patricia Gomez lived nearby. They continued to believe Castro's claims, but both Mona and Patricia met other men and would get engaged—not before Castro talked Mona into taking out a $750,000 life insurance policy that named her daughter as the beneficiary and Patricia as her daughter's caregiver. Then tragedy struck. Mona, with her daughter and fiancé, Jim, who held a pilot's license, set off on a short flight, but the small aircraft went missing. This left Castro and Patricia to try to cash in the insurance policy. At first they were thwarted due to no bodies being found, but when the wreckage and all three bodies were discovered, the insurance firm paid out.

In 2001, Castro, Patricia, her new husband, their young child, and a girlfriend of Castro's called K.L. all moved to Wichita, buying properties in K.L.'s name. Real-estate agent Jennifer Huston had helped the group buy property and became close to Castro, so much so that she left her husband and moved in with the group, bringing her two daughters, Emily, aged 10, and Sarah, aged 17. The young girls continued to be told that Perez was a magical man with mystic powers, possessed by angels, claims substantiated by Patricia. With a bigger plot of land purchased in Sedgwick County, Kansas, Detective Goodwyn's attention was drawn to the group called "Angel's Landing."

MURDER FOR MONEY

Angel's Landing was, in many ways, a popular group, even entertaining police officers at their many parties and barbecues. What Goodwyn noticed,

Castro's victims took out several insurance policies, which he quickly cashed in after their deaths.

however, was the number of luxury vehicles the group possessed, and the extent to which Castro could afford to indulge his passion for collecting model airplanes. Seemingly the group were living a lavish lifestyle, full of luxury. They had a big home, land, and a swimming pool, but what was going on behind closed doors was depraved and tragic. Castro had continued to tell his followers that he needed pure, young girls to share his bed or else he would die. Emily was forced to sleep with Castro aged only 10, and like her older sister, was repeatedly raped.

Castro would turn violent, blaming one of the angels possessing him, and often the women would be held at gunpoint, forced to "step up," as he would put it. Soon, with money seemingly running out, Castro decided that it was time to cash in another insurance policy; this time, that of his oldest follower, Patricia. Emily would later testify that Castro came to her, saying it was soon Patricia's "time to go" and to tell the authorities that they saw Patricia run to the pool to help her struggling young daughter but fell, hit her head, and drowned.

Paramedics and the police believed the group's account of Patricia's death. She had a blunt-force injury to her head, and her death was deemed a tragic accident. In August 2003, the policy paid out to her husband, Brian Hughes, who was still part of the cult. More vehicles were bought for all the members.

Angel's Landing grew as new members joined, relationships formed, and life insurance policies were taken out, all under the careful eye of Castro. But, by now, he too was being watched.

In February 2015, Castro was finally sentenced to eighty years in prison for his crimes.

FINALLY STOPPED

Castro felt that the police might have their suspicions about what went on inside his compound. To curry favor with them, he donated $19,000 to the local sheriff's office for a new vehicle, but this didn't deter Detective Goodwyn, who continued to gather evidence on a man with seemingly no past. Goodwyn presumed Castro must be involved in drugs, but when Brian Hughes, a skilled mechanic, was crushed by a car he was working under, and the detective came across the obituary for Mona Griffith and her family, he began to wonder whether the leader was guilty of murder. In the meantime, Brian's insurance policy paid out and the group's finances were supplemented once again.

Looking into the group's financial affairs, Goodwyn ascertained that whenever the bank balance was low—around every two-and-a-half years—a member would be killed and their policy would pay out. He couldn't charge anyone yet as this was just a theory, but when Sarah and Emily's mother, Jennifer, committed suicide by driving her car head-on into a truck, he was convinced that she had been talked into taking her own life by Castro.

The detective started to visit the compound regularly, trying to get a fingerprint from Castro. But the cult leader wasn't to be fooled and soon left Kansas for Tennessee, where he created a new pseudonym. By now the FBI had been informed and started their own investigation. They had evidence of the leader, now going under the name Joe Venegas, committing identity theft, and with a fingerprint taken on arrest, they discovered he was, in fact, Daniel Perez.

While Perez served time for fraud, the police and the FBI further investigated the cult and interviewed Sarah and Emily who now, as young adults, testified to the abuse they suffered, and in Emily's case, the fact that she was told by Castro to lie about the circumstances of Patricia's death. On September 11, 2011, Perez was charged with several crimes that included first-degree murder, rape, and aggravated sexual assault. Various members (among them Sarah and Emily) testified, and in February 2015, Perez was found guilty on all counts, including the murder of Patricia. He was imprisoned for eighty years.

CASE NOTES: TRAINEE SLEUTH

In her early twenties, Sarah became more independent and started dating a trainee policeman called Daniel McGrath. Daniel had begun to have his suspicions of the group and its leader. While doing some digging, he persuaded Sarah to tell him the truth. Sarah went into detail about how Angel's Landing had been subsidized by insurance payouts and that its leader had been raping her and other minors for years. Daniel convinced Sarah to let him report this to the police and the FBI, and when interviewed by Detective Goodwyn he was able to tip off the authorities that their suspect had moved to Colombia in Tennessee, where they arrested him initially for identity theft. Today, Sarah and Daniel are married.

SARAH LAWRENCE COLLEGE CULT

LOCATION:............BRONXVILLE AND NEW YORK
CITY, NEW YORK, USA

YEARS ACTIVE:.......................................2010-20

FOUNDER:...LARRY RAY

Larry Ray moved into his daughter's college dorm, where he proceeded
to create an abusive sex cult that ruined the lives of her housemates.
Ray exuded authority; if they had a problem, he told them he could
solve it. After gaining the students' trust, he began to degrade them
through constant psychological manipulation and physical abuse.

In September 2010, at the start of her sophomore year, Talia Ray
moved into the Slonim Woods dorm building at Sarah Lawrence,
a prestigious liberal arts college in Bronxville, just north of New York
City. During her freshman year, she had regularly talked about her
father, Larry, who she described in glowing terms, so when she
announced he was going to crash in her dorm room, her seven
housemates did not object. Ray had just been released from prison,
but Talia shrouded him in mystery, telling her housemates he had
worked for the CIA and moved among the Manhattan elite.

A sex cult was set up in the unlikely surroundings of the prestigious Sarah Lawrence College.

After his arrival, Ray began to hang out in the dorm's common areas, sharing wildly exaggerated stories with the housemates about how he knew world leaders and had helped bring peace to war-torn Kosovo. They were intrigued. "I thought it was the coolest thing ever," said housemate Santos Rosario, while Daniel Levin said, "All I wanted was to be like him." Ray began to host "family dinners" and "house meetings" in which he introduced them to his program for personal transformation called "Quest for Potential." He offered "therapy sessions," for which he had no qualifications, but students opened up and shared their stories with him.

"It was through these 'sessions' Ray laid the groundwork for psychological conditioning that would eventually lead these young adults to become unwitting victims of sexual exploitation, verbal and physical abuse, extortion, forced labor, and prostitution," said FBI Assistant Director in Charge William F. Sweeney, Jr.

A CHAMELEON

Born in 1959, Ray has been described as a "chameleon" who had worked on Wall Street and owned an Italian restaurant and a nightclub in New Jersey. He also served in the Air Force, but only for nineteen days. Ray had lived on the periphery of power and celebrity, being the best man of the infamous New York police commissioner Bernie Kerik, who later described him as "psychotic conman," and also once provided security for the former Soviet leader Mikhail Gorbachev on a visit to New York. In 2003, Ray was convicted of securities fraud and given five years' probation, which he violated when he was arrested for domestic violence and jailed for three years. Within days of his release, he began living with his daughter at Sarah Lawrence.

CAMPAIGN OF VIOLENCE AND EXTORTION

During the housemates' "therapy sessions" Ray forced them to make bogus confessions, telling them they had damaged his property and had to pay vast amounts of money. "They'd become profit centers," said former FBI agent Frank Figliuzzi. "He has them drain bank accounts of their parents, in some cases, their life savings because they convinced their parents, 'I have done some damage, I owe this guy money, I'm in big trouble.'"

During the summer of 2011, and for several years thereafter, many of the students stayed at Ray's apartment on the Upper East Side in Manhattan. They also stayed with him after they had graduated, and Rosario's sisters, Felicia and Yalitza, who had not attended Sarah Lawrence, fell under his spell and moved into the apartment. Ray inflicted sleep deprivation, denied them food, and ruled with a constant threat of violence. "He drove me to attempt suicide more than once," said Rosario.

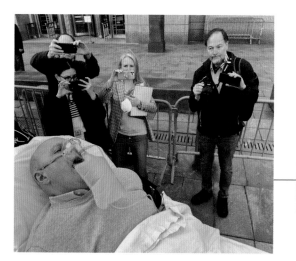

Ray is wheeled out of court into an ambulance in New York City on March 22, 2022.

BROUGHT DOWN BY *NEW YORK MAGAZINE*

Some members left, but Claudia Drury (see Case Notes, below) continued to be sex trafficked by Ray, helped by housemate Isabella Pollock. Drury eventually freed herself after confessing to a client she had been forced into sex work.

In April 2019, *New York Magazine* published a feature entitled, "The Stolen Kids of Sarah Lawrence." This led to an investigation and Ray's eventual arrest in 2020. In September 2022, he was found guilty on fifteen counts, including extortion, racketeering, conspiracy, forced labor, and sex trafficking, and was sentenced to sixty years in prison. Judge Lewis Liman called him an "evil genius" and that he had "sought to take every bit of light from his victims' lives. It was sadism, pure and simple."

In 2023, Pollock, the only housemate who was a willing participant, was sentenced to four and a half years in prison for participating in a money laundering scheme.

CASE NOTES:
THE PROSTITUTION OF CLAUDIA DRURY

Ray extorted the most money from Claudia Drury, up to $2.5 million over seven years. He convinced her that she had tried to poison him, taping a confession to blackmail her into working as a sex worker charging up to $8,000 for an evening.

"It was unrelenting sadism," Drury said. "It was hell, and it was a deliberate, educated, and sustained campaign to break me. Every time I was forced to prostitute myself . . . I felt myself getting more numb." Drury has also recounted Ray's violence. "He slapped me in the face so hard I fell over, [he] pulled my hair, strangled me, suffocated me, hit me. He threatened to put me in jail numerous times."

3

FUNDAMENTALIST
CULTS

These are the cults that want to
break from convention and pursue
a radical fundamentalist approach.
We look at five, including the
Fundamentalist Church of Jesus
Christ of Latter-Day Saints,
who splintered from the original
church so they could continue to
practice polygamy. Their leader
Warren Jeffs took this to extremes
by taking seventy-eight wives and
having sixty children.

UNIFICATION
CHURCH

LOCATION:................(FORMED) SEOUL, SOUTH
KOREA; NOW WORLDWIDE

YEARS ACTIVE:.................... 1954-PRESENT DAY

FOUNDERE: .... SUN MYUNG MOON

They were set up to purify the human race. They were set up to bring mankind back from a shameful past. Their leader was the new "Messiah," and over decades, he and his group amassed hundreds of thousands of followers. With a holy emphasis on marriage, mass weddings (one included 20,000 participants) are a mainstay, but away from the white dresses and promises of eternal love, the Unification Church might not be all it seems.

Moon would deliver speeches to thousands of followers; his mission, to purify the world.

Sun Myung Moon was born in Sangsa-ri in what is now North Korea in 1920. When he was 10, his family converted to Christianity, having formerly followed Confucianist beliefs. Moon attended Sunday school at Presbyterian church and began preaching after World War II. After being incarcerated by the North Koreans for alleged spying, Moon moved to Seoul and it was there, in 1954, that he founded The Holy Spirit Association for the Unification of World Christianity (HSA-UWC).

Expanding quickly, after a year it had thirty centers around South Korea before spreading further around East Asia. The next twenty years saw the church grow across continents. Missionaries were sent to Europe in the late 1960s, and by the 1970s groups were being formed in the USA. Moon himself moved to America in 1971. He remained a citizen of South Korea but his influence in the USA was growing rapidly, underlined by the series of speeches he gave at New York's Maddison Square Gardens and the Yankee Stadium, and in front of 300,000 people at Washington, D.C.'s Monument Grounds, in which he named his address "God's Hope for America."

In the USA, suspicions were raised that members were being pressurized into offering vast financial donations, and that they were being "brainwashed." The authorities were so convinced of this manipulation that in 1976, the HSA-UWC leader in the USA had to meet with Senator Bob Dole to placate any federal fears. Interest in the group had grown more widespread across the globe a year earlier when 1.2 million people attended an HSA-UWC event in Yeouido, South Korea.

Through the 1980s, the church continued to grow, in numbers and influence. Moon advocated his American followers to reach out and recruit neighbors, In May 1994, Moon changed the name of his church to Family Federation for World Peace and Unification (known widely as the Unification Church) and stated that it now worked with other global religious institutes to eradicate "sinful activity" such as sexual immorality and homosexuality.

BELIEFS

Moon's church was tied loosely to Judaeo-Christian tradition, preaching that humankind had fallen from grace when Adam and Eve disobeyed God's commands and that because of their fornication, mankind had become the "children of Satan." Moon felt that the Bible needed to be reinterpreted and just three years after forming the church, he published *Exposition of the Divine Principle*. The book taught that God is all-powerful and all-knowing but has to be "humanized" because he cannot be complete without the reciprocal love of his children. God's original plan was that men and women are deemed to be sons and daughters of God, just as Jesus was God's son, and that if Adam and Eve had not fallen, "All men and women would have been of the same perfection as Jesus." Moon advocated that all men and women should "become Messiahs" (persons who are one in mind and body with God); and that all of God's work in history is to establish the family with God at its core. The church went on to teach that the family is the foothold in which humankind will redeem all their past mistakes.

The church also believed in the principle of restoration, meaning that the purpose of creation was to build the Kingdom of Heaven on Earth, and that it will be God who ultimately saves a sinful world and restores it to its purest state. The church teaches that throughout history, and since Adam and Eve, God has tried to save this sinful world. First through Noah and the flood, but Noah's son Ham sinned once more, and then through Jesus Christ, a Messiah sent to create the perfect family, but who once again was thwarted when man crucified him.

Moon taught that in these "Last Days" a second Messiah would come, the Messiah would be successful and "the true parents of humanity" would fulfill the purpose of creationism. Followers of the church believed Moon and his second wife, Hak Ja Han, to be those "true parents."

MASS WEDDINGS

In 1961, Moon arranged his first mass wedding ceremony. In Seoul, thirty-six couples, twenty-four of whom were matched by Moon, were married or had their vows renewed in order to remove themselves from the lineage of human sin, keeping in line with the belief that Eve had been seduced by Satan and therefore the human bloodline had been contaminated ever since.

Since then, these mass wedding gatherings have grown bigger, so big that in 1997, a reported 28,000 couples met in what was called "a marriage affirmation ceremony." The church refuses to give its blessing to same-sex couples, and with other beliefs, including the abstinence of sex outside of marriage, is said to side with evangelical Christianity.

In 1997, 28,000 couples were wed in one ceremony of the church's multiple mass weddings.

CONTROVERSIES

Reverend Moon was convicted of tax evasion in 1982. Many of his supporters, including mainstream religious leaders, felt that the trial was merely an example of governmental religious prejudice, but the affair cast further shadows over the institute's methods and motives. The act of matching couples and marrying them raised particular suspicions, and while many of the mass ceremonies were not legal weddings (couples would often be married after the ceremonies), the church was criticized for placing under-age girls into marriages.

Moon's own son was matched with a 15-year-old Korean girl named Nansook Hong, who in 1998 published a book called *In the Shadow of the Moons*, in which she described the abusive marriage she was forced into as a teenager, and the vast amounts of cash donated to Moon. Hong went on to describe how Moon proclaimed himself and his family to be perfect but in fact his son, her husband, was a drug addict who physically abused her.

Other members (predominantly wives in arranged marriages) have complained of being brainwashed. Away from the marriages, critics have suggested the church, far from being a religious institute, is in fact big business which, according to an article in the English newspaper the *Financial Times* in 2022, has multibillion-dollar interests "ranging from a Brazilian football club to a Californian chinchilla ranch."

Religiously, the church's belief that Jesus should have married and that events such as both world wars and the Holocaust were necessary in order to establish the Kingdom of God have brought further censure. Politically, the church has also received criticism. In 1998, the Egyptian newspaper *Al-Ahram* criticized Moon's "ultra-right leanings" and suggested he had a personal relationship with the then conservative Israeli prime minister Benjamin Netanyahu, accusing them of being fervently anti-Arab.

Moon himself died in 2012, and his death saw the church splinter into several factions, each run by his wife and various sons.

The 2022 assassination
of the Japanese prime
minister Shinzo Abe
shocked the world.

CASE NOTES: ASSASSINATION

Despite the country not being a vastly religious one, the Unification Church enjoyed considerable success in Japan. However, when in 2022 Japanese prime minister Shinzo Abe was assassinated, a light was shone on the church and questions were asked about the influence it had on its followers.

The man accused of shooting Abe, Tetsuya Yamagami, stated that the assassination was a revenge attack against the Unification Church, an institute he blamed for impoverishing himself and his family. Yamagami's mother had joined the church but had allegedly been pressurized into donating $720,000 to its funds.

Yamagami declared that he had planned to kill Moon's wife, Hak Ja Han, but he couldn't get near enough to her. Instead he chose Abe, who although never a member of the church, had publicly praised its activities, and it was also thought that his grandfather, Japan's former prime minister Nobusuke Kishi, had paved the way for Moon's fiercely anticommunist church to gain a foothold in Japan.

FLDS

LOCATION:................UTAH AND ARIZONA, USA

YEARS ACTIVE:....................... 2002-11

FOUNDER:...................... RULON JEFFS

The polygamist cult leader Warren Jeffs reportedly had a total of
seventy-eight wives and sixty children. He was seen as the prophet
who could never be wrong, the one whose word must be obeyed.
He succeeded his father as leader of the Fundamentalist Church of
Jesus Christ of Latter-Day Saints (FLDS), having been anointed as the
"chosen vessel," and married all but two of his father's sixty-five wives.

Growing up in the FLDS, Warren Jeffs was always made to feel special. The president of the church and his father, Rulon Jeffs, may have had a total of sixty children, but he anointed his son Warren as his successor.

"My father said that Warren was a very special person, and was brought here by God for a specific reason," said his half-brother Wallace Jeffs. "We were expected to revere him, as he would be our next prophet."

Born in 1955, Warren was appointed principal of the FLDS's private school Alta Academy at the age of only 20. He ruled the school with what Wallace has called "a reign of terror . . . he was a monster," as he sexually abused the children in his care.

When his father, who reportedly had sixty-five wives, died in 2002, Jeffs took over as president of the FLDS church, with his full title being "President and Prophet, Seer and Revelator." There were 15,000 members living in several communities, mainly in Hildale, Utah, and just across the border in Colorado City, Arizona, which is collectively known as Short Creek.

The FLDS's 15,000 members lived together at Short Creek, which spanned the border of Arizona and Utah.

The FLDS is a denomination of Mormonism and a splinter group from the original Church of Jesus Christ of the Latter-Day Saints, which first issued a manifesto ending polygamy in 1890. By the 1930s, a Mormon community in Short Creek were refusing to renounce the practice of polygamy and so were excommunicated from the main LDS church.

The FLDS believe that polygamy, also known as plural marriage, is a means to gain salvation for male members. Jeffs claimed that a man needed at least three wives to get into heaven, but the more wives he has, the closer he is to getting there.

SEVENTY-EIGHT WIVES

When Jeffs took over the church he said, "I won't say much, but I will say hands off my father's wives." Within a week he had married all but two of them, with one refusing and one escaping from the community. Now as church president, Jeffs had seventy-eight wives, including twenty-four who were underage children, some as young as 12 years old.

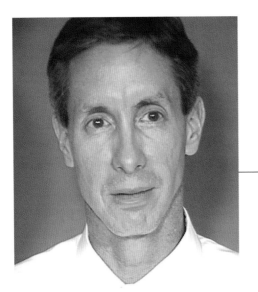

Jeffs was sentenced to life in prison in August 2011 for the aggravated sexual assault of two girls aged 12 and 15.

Elissa Wall was born into the community and at the age of 14 was forced to marry her 19-year-old cousin, Allen Steed. "I really think it was about submission," she has said. "I could have become a really big problem for the community and Warren. I was a little more outspoken than the average girl. But I think it was about pounding me into submission . . . I was just the next player he wanted to quickly get control over."

"I was now the property of my cousin. And no matter how resistant I was to him, his job was to get me into submission as quickly as possible."

Warren Jeffs was the only one in the community who could perform marriages and assign wives to men, effectively forcing any woman into a marriage. He could also take a woman away from her husband and reassign her to another man.

"A MONSTER AND A PEDOPHILE"

Jeffs' reign began to crumble in June 2004 when his nephew Brent Jeffs filed a civil lawsuit alleging he had been sexually assaulted by him as a child in the 1980s. "He was a monster and a pedophile," he said.

In June 2005, Jeffs was charged in Mohave County, Arizona, with sexual assault on a minor and conspiracy to commit sexual misconduct with a minor by arranging the marriage between Wall and Steed. Jeffs went on the run, while the Arizona authorities distributed "Wanted" posters and offered a $10,000 reward.

While he was a fugitive, Utah issued a new arrest warrant for him on charges of being an accomplice in the rape of a teenage girl. The FBI now became involved and placed him on their Top Ten Most Wanted Fugitives list, with a reward of $100,000. It was believed that while on the run, Jeffs secretly returned to Colorado City in order to perform more marriages with underage children.

On August 28, 2006, Jeffs was pulled over close to Las Vegas in Clark County, Nevada, by a highway trooper who noticed the license plates on his Cadillac Escalade were not visible. Inside the car with Jeffs was one of his wives, Naomi Jessop, and his brother Isaac. Police also found computers, cell phones, numerous disguises, and $55,000 in cash.

Jeffs faced the Utah charges first, and on September 25, 2007, was found guilty on two counts of being an accomplice to rape and sentenced to ten years to life. Three years later, the Utah Supreme Court overturned the conviction after finding fault with the instructions given to the jury during his trial. In 2010, the Arizona authorities dismissed their charges against him, as the victims no longer wished to testify.

However, Jeffs had also been charged with aggravated sexual assault on two girls, aged 12 and 15, who he had taken as his wives. On August 9, 2011, after a trial in San Angelo, Texas, Jeffs was convicted and sentenced to life in prison. "He used his position of authority to corrupt and pervert . . . a religion, to continue his victimization of women and children," said the prosecutor Eric Nichols after the verdict.

Jeffs had hidden behind the mask of religion to "corrupt and pevert."

Women in the
FLDS community were
forced to play a
submissive role.

CASE NOTES:
LIFE INSIDE THE FLDS COMMUNITY

"I thought that I was blessed because I happened to be born into the FLDS," said Faith Bistline, who escaped from it in 2011. "We were always told that it was very wicked outside, I thought that normal people were miserable with their lives."

But inside the community women had almost no control over their lives. They were forced into marriage, then expected to blindly serve their husbands and not complain if they took more wives. The women were made to wear long prairie-style dresses, keep their hair long, have it styled into a quiff, and not wear any makeup.

"We didn't interact with the outside world," Elissa Wall said. "We didn't go to public school. We were educated, cultivated, and bred to be products of the church and the religion." There was also no television, no radio, and no internet allowed. "Jeffs said media was Satan's tool," Wallace Jeffs said.

SCHOOL OF
PROPHETS

LOCATION:..........AMERICAN FORK, UTAH, USA

YEARS ACTIVE:...1984

FOUNDERS:...................RON AND DAN LAFFERTY

A sleepy town in rural America. A community that thrived on closeness, where neighbors looked out for one another and doors could be kept unlocked. At the heart of that community was religion; the bedrock of the people's beliefs and a constant in their lives. But when a husband came home to find his wife and their 15-month-old baby brutally murdered, that community and the religion on which so much of it was built fell apart.

The Laffertys were a hard-working church-going family. Watson and Claudine Lafferty had been married in 1940 and had eight children, six of them boys. Devout members of The Church of Jesus Christ of Latter-Day Saints, or Mormons, as they are commonly known, the couple brought up their children in a similar fashion. Watson was a chiropractor, and while he instilled a stringent work ethic in his children, he was also fervently against the federal government and had strong views on modern medicine. His religious beliefs became extreme. When one son accidentally shot himself in the stomach with a bow and arrow, he told him that he would have to suffer in silence until the morning as penance for breaking the Sabbath.

The boys, including Ron (the eldest) and Dan, shared their father's extreme religious beliefs. Both moved away from Utah to go on missions, as was the practice. Having returned as missionaries, each brother was married. These were respected men but their stances concerning the Mormon Church became increasingly radical.

Dan and his wife, Matilda, had started their own sandwich business. It was successful, but when the Internal Revenue Service and the Health Department forced them to close, Dan became increasingly detached, and, like his father, paranoid about the federal government. His brother, Ron, shared these fervent beliefs and with their mutual fundamentalism, it wasn't long before each of their families and their church grew concerned.

The Laffertys' extremism saw them excommunicated by the Mormon Church.

One of Dan Lafferty's strong convictions was for the practice of polygamy. The Mormon Church had banned polygamy in 1890, but among fundamentalist believers, having more than one wife was seen as a religious right. When, in 1982, Dan tried to take his 14-year-old stepdaughter as his second wife, he was excommunicated from the Mormon Church. A year later, Ron left too. Again, he was excommunicated for his ever-growing extremism, which included that same embracing of polygamy. Outcast from their church, Ron and Dan joined the School of Prophets. Founded and run by the Prophet Onias, aka Bob Crossfield, in the town of American Fork, the breakaway sect shared their fundamentalist beliefs, and soon both Ron and Dan were taking meetings in their own homes.

Dan's daughter, Rebecca, who was seven at the time, recalls that "The School of Prophets was a cult. I remember them bringing in a pulpit and speaking in our home. It was very hush-hush, and just weird." Soon "weird" would turn into horrific.

A MURDEROUS SECT

Small groups would meet at one another's homes, and with the vast majority of them men, the concept of polygamy was a main focus. Communication with God is among the core beliefs of the Mormon Church, and Bob Crossfield would train the group's followers so that they too could receive these revelations from God. In 1984, Ron, by now one of the leaders of the group, reported that he had begun to receive messages "in earnest." One of them he called the "removal revelation," and within this handwritten note that he showed to other cult members were instructions from heaven that Brenda, the wife of his younger brother, Allen, and their baby daughter, Erica, should be killed.

Both Ron and Dan's wives were fervently antipolygamy, and when they had consulted Brenda Lafferty, a strong and independent woman, she adamantly argued that they should by no means tolerate being in plural marriages. Along with Brenda, the "removal revelation" commanded that Richard Stowe, a prominent figure who presided over the brothers' excommunication, plus Chloe Low, who aided Ron's wife's divorce, should also be "removed."

Ron Lafferty told followers he had received revelations direct from God and heaven.

When Allen Lafferty was told of the revelation, he didn't tell his wife because he didn't want to worry her, and while he was concerned with how extreme his brothers had become at the School of Prophets, he couldn't believe they would murder anyone. But, with both Ron and Dan's wives having left them, the two men became more certain of the revelation, and began to plot a horrific murder.

On July 24, 1984, Ron and Dan Lafferty, with two acquaintances, drifters called "Chip" Carnes and Richard Knapp, filled their car with shotguns and knives and headed to their youngest brother's home. Allen Lafferty was working 70 miles (112 kilometers) away that day and had called his wife at lunchtime to say hello to her and Erica. It was the last time he spoke to either of them.

That afternoon, Ron and Dan knocked on Brenda's door, forced their way past her, brutally attacked her, and killed her and her daughter by cutting their throats. Carnes and Knapp had been in the car when the attacks happened, and despite being horrified at seeing the brothers covered in blood, they drove with them to Chloe Low's home. Fortunately, their target was away on vacation. They burglarized the house and carried on. After missing the turning to Richard Stowe's home, and with their "revelation" half carried out, they left town.

Ron Lafferty (center) is escorted from the Utah County Court House on April 25, 1985.

When Allen returned home from work to find the most horrific of scenes, he hurried to his neighbor, phoned the police, and while he was being interviewed about his family's murders, he informed the officers about his brothers' motives. Immediately, the hunt was on to find them.

The car the brothers had driven was located by the FBI in Wyoming, but only Knapp and Carnes were found. They had stolen the car from the Laffertys but told officers where they had disposed of the knife used, and when, almost a month after the murders, FBI agents were tipped off that the brothers were in Reno, they were arrested at a casino. All four men were charged with two counts of criminal homicide.

THE TRIAL

Both Knapp and Carnes had their charges dropped but testified against the brothers at the trial that took place in 1985. Ron Lafferty had tried to kill himself in December 1984, but despite his injuries and mental state was deemed fit for trial. During the hearings, there were conflicting reports on which brother carried out the murders. Dan stated that he killed both, but Carnes and Knapp stated that Ron had killed Brenda, and thanked Dan for "doing the baby."

The brothers were tried separately, both were found guilty, but in Dan's case the jury could not unanimously vote for the death penalty, so he was sentenced to life in prison instead. Ron was sentenced to death. His conviction was overturned in 1991, but five years later he was retried and again sentenced to death.

While Dan remains in prison today, Ron was scheduled to be executed in 2020 but died of natural causes in 2019, his thirty-four years in prison making him one of the longest-serving condemned inmates in the country.

CASE NOTES:
THE DAVID FAMILY MASS SUICIDE

In 1978, Immanuel David, formerly known as Charles Longo, took his large family to live in a Salt Lake hotel. By now, David, a devout member and (like Ron and Dan Lafferty) a returned missionary of The Church of Jesus Christ of Latter-Day Saints, had been excommunicated, but along with a group of followers, decreed that he was in fact God, Jesus Christ, *and* the Holy Ghost. He changed his name, after which his family and followers called themselves the Family of David.

David was being indicted by the FBI for fraud when he killed himself in July of that year. His wife, Rachel, under his instruction, took all seven of their children to the roof of the hotel and threw them off, before jumping the eleven stories to her death. Her oldest child, Rachel, then 15, was the only survivor, and confined to a wheelchair as a result of her injuries. She remained adamant that her father was God and that one day he would return to Earth. "I remember my father said he will be back. I know he will," she told reporters in 1993. "My father never lied."

THE KIRTLAND CULT

LOCATION:......................KIRTLAND, OHIO, USA

YEARS ACTIVE:.. 1984-90

FOUNDER:............................ JEFFREY LUNDGREN

Jeffrey Lundgren convinced his followers he was a prophet who could talk to God; they called him "Dad," handed over their money, and obeyed his every word. Their faith in Lundgren was so strong, followers believed his claim that the only way they could be brought before God was by committing a "blood sacrifice," the murder of an innocent family.

Lundgren worked as a tour guide at the RLDS's Kirtland Temple in Kirtland, Ohio.

Born on May 3, 1950, in Independence, Missouri, Lundgren was raised as a member of the Reorganized Church of Jesus Christ of Latter-Day Saints (RLDS), an offshoot of the Latter-Day Saints Church. Lundgren grew up with a strict and abusive father. As a teenager, he became a keen hunter and acquired a thorough knowledge of firearms. He left home to study at Central Missouri State University, where he met fellow student Alice Keeler. It was noted how controlling he was toward Alice, who he asked to marry just a week after their first date. He would skip classes to stare into the window of her classes until he was kicked out of the university.

In 1970, Lundgren married Alice and enlisted in the navy, spending time on active duty in the Vietnam War before being honorably discharged after four years. He then drifted through life, struggling to support his growing family, which soon included four children. In the early 1980s, Lundgren returned to the RLDS in Independence to fulfill his desire to become a priest. Once ordained, he preached about how God's wrath would destroy the wicked but was soon sacked for his harsh fundamentalism. In April 1984, Lundgren declared God had told him to move to Kirtland to set up his own church.

After arriving, he became a tour guide at the RLDS's Kirtland Temple. He hosted Bible classes in which he built a small, loyal band of fundamentalists, who shared his hatred of the church's liberalization and recent decision to allow women priests.

In October 1987, the Kirtland Temple sacked Lundgren after discovering he had stolen an estimated $40,000 of contributions from visitors. He moved to a farmhouse on the edge of Kirtland, setting up a group with around twelve followers. He proclaimed himself a prophet who spoke directly to God, declaring the main RLDS was overrun with sinners, and the only way to get to heaven was to stay with him. At the farmhouse, Lundgren hosted nightly Bible talks as he gained more control over his followers' lives, emotionally and financially. The Avery family had been so entranced by Lundgren they sold their house in Independence, followed him over 800 miles (1,300 kilometers) across the country to live in Kirtland, and gave him a lump sum of $10,000.

Lundgren started planning a violent takeover of the RLDS church in Kirtland and the murder of its pastor, Reverend Dale Luffman, who he said he wanted to publicly execute by cutting off his head. The date was set for May 3, 1988, and some of his followers began stockpiling weapons and practicing military maneuvers in the grounds of the farmhouse. Alarmed follower Kevin Currie fled to Buffalo, New York, and told the FBI about these plans. The information was passed to the local Kirtland police, who placed Lundgren under surveillance, which forced him to reluctantly ditch his plot.

THE BLOOD SACRIFICE

By the end of 1988, Lundgren began to tell his followers they would have to make a "blood sacrifice" if they wanted to be brought before God. He had to kill the sinners among them, otherwise God would strike down the entire group. They could only see God after he had made this killing.

Lundgren chose Dennis Avery and his family to be his victims. He had never warmed to Avery, and felt his wife Cheryl wielded too much power, even though they both worshipped him. "[His followers] told us they had to do [the murders] for religious reasons," assistant county prosecutor Karen Kowall said.

On April 10, 1989, some of Lundgren's followers began digging a 3 foot-(1 meter-) deep hole inside the barn next to the farmhouse. On the evening of April 17, after they had spent the day together, Lundgren asked Dennis if he would come to see something inside the barn. Once he stepped inside, Dennis was wrestled to the floor as he shouted, "Please, this isn't necessary!" before having his hands and feet tied together. He was thrown into the pit and shot twice in the back. A follower beckoned Cheryl into the barn, telling her Dennis needed help with something, before she too was bound, thrown in the pit, and shot three times. The girls, 15-year-old Trina, 13-year-old Rebecca, and 7-year-old Karen, were each taken to the barn and shot dead. Lundgren returned to the farmhouse and announced, "It is done . . . It was God's will," before followers filled in the hole, covered it with trash, and sprinkled it with lime to disguise the smell.

The next day, sixteen FBI agents and the local police came to the farmhouse, with no idea five murders had just taken place. They had instead come to talk about the aborted church takeover and left without making any arrests.

Lundgren led a small but loyal band of followers from a farmhouse on the outskirts of Kirtland, Ohio.

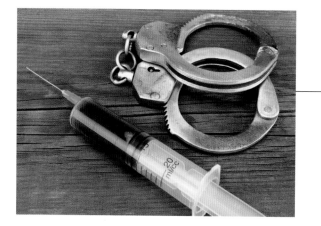

Lundgren was executed by lethal injection on October 24, 2006.

DOWNFALL

On April 18, 1989, the group fled to a campsite in the Appalachian Mountains in West Virginia. Lundgren called it "The Wilderness," where they would all be absolved of their sins. He told them God was delighted with their "blood sacrifice," and he now wanted to be known as "God of the Whole Life." But the group was starting to fragment, with followers realizing he was a false prophet and repulsed at the murder of three children. Many drifted away, and Lundgren took his family to California.

There were no reports that the Avery family were missing; it was assumed they had moved to another town. This was until December 31, 1989, when one of Lundgren's followers, Keith Johnson, sought revenge as Lundgren had taken his wife Kathy as a second wife. He told the Bureau of Alcohol, Tobacco, Firearms, and Explosives in Kansas City, Missouri, about the murders and provided them with a hand-drawn map to find the bodies. On January 3 and 4, 1990, a team of police officers removed layers of trash piled on top of the grave and excavated soil to find the bodies of the Avery family. "The smell of death hung in the air." This was the abiding memory of Lake County prosecutor Steve LaTourette. Their bodies had been there for some time, and it was clear they had all been tied up and shot. There were garbage bags in the pit containing the family's belongings, including the girls' drawings and notebooks. "There were some pretty seasoned law enforcement officers there that day, and I remember the effect it had on them when it was clear the children had been murdered," Kowall recalled.

The Kirtland police knew immediately who was responsible for this horrific scene as they already had a bulging file on him: the former tenant, Jeffrey Lundgren. After his arrest near San Diego (see Case Notes, below), on August 29, 1990, Lundgren was found guilty and sentenced to death for five counts of murder and kidnap. His defense lawyers wanted him to plead insanity but he refused. Alice was sentenced to 150 years, and their son Damon Lundgren to 120 years. At his sentencing Lundgren insisted, "It's not a figment of my imagination, I can talk to God."

Within a week the police had rounded up all his followers. Ronald Luff, who said the Averys were "truly good people" but that Lundgren had been "mandated by God" to kill them, was sentenced to up to 170 years, Daniel Kraft to fifty years, while Richard Brand, Gregory Winship, Sharon Bluntschly, Susan Luff, and Deborah Olivarez spent twenty years in prison before their release in 2010 and 2011. A handful of followers with more minor roles were each sentenced to a year in prison. On October 24, 2006, Lundgren was executed by lethal injection at the Southern Ohio Correctional Facility in Lucasville.

CASE NOTES: CAPTURED IN CALIFORNIA

On January 4, 1990, while staying at a motel in San Diego, California, Lundgren learned from a television report the police had discovered the bodies in the barn and that he was the prime suspect.

Later that day, he made a call from a payphone to Alice's mother to come and collect his youngest three children, before he, Alice, and their eldest son Damon went into hiding. But the police had tapped the mother's phone. This led them to the payphone near San Diego, which they staked out, and on January 7, they arrested the Lundgren family in room 29 at the Sante Fe Motel.

TRUE RUSSIAN
ORTHODOX CHURCH

LOCATION:.................................. PENZA, RUSSIA

YEARS ACTIVE:.. 2006-08

FOUNDER:................................... PYOTR KUZNETSOV

He took them away from their church. He told them that their old beliefs were far from sufficient, and that the end of the world would soon be upon us all. Having manipulated the way they lived their lives, including what they ate and how they spent their money, their leader ordered them to build and live in a cave. There, they would wait for the end of times.

Pyotr Kuznetsov was born in 1964, in Belarus, then part of the Soviet Union. Like much of the population, he followed the Russian Orthodox Church (ROC), one of the largest independent Eastern Orthodox faiths in the world. Under Communist rule, the influence of the Russian church had fluctuated. However, the collapse of the Soviet Union in 1991 strengthened the church and by 2007, the ROC enjoyed great support and authority.

However, by that time Kuznetsov had become increasingly dissatisfied with the ROC. The word "orthodox" stems from the Greek words "Ortho" and "Doxa," meaning "straight opinion," or "true faith." For Kuznetsov, his beliefs became stronger, and he felt that the ROC was, in fact, not true, and certainly not orthodox enough. He felt that the church was not telling its people the truth or preparing them for what was coming, and having left his work as an engineer and his home in Belarus, he began to travel across Russia.

Kuznetsov made his way around the country, trying to spread his new take on the religion. Through books, articles, and by touring monasteries, he cited the end of the world as a looming catastrophe, and in time he had garnered

Kuznetsov was dissatisfied with the teachings of the Russian Orthodox Church.

Members of the cult
leave the cave in which
they were living, in
April, 2008.

several dozen followers. In 2006, he took his group with him to a small village called Nikolskoye in the Penza region of central Russia, where they settled. As the group did not have a name (other than "The Chosen Ones"), some began to call them "The True Russian Orthodox Church," and as they became increasingly introverted, shut away from the rest of society, they were also known as "The Penza Recluses."

CAVE DWELLERS

Having settled in the small village, to the locals they came across as merely a shy and slightly eccentric religious group. A modest tin-roofed prayer hall was where they convened to sing their songs and say their prayers. "They are simple Christians," Father Georgy, a local priest, told a TV channel. "They say: 'The church is doing a bad job, the end of the world is coming soon and we are all saving ourselves.'"

Behind closed doors, the idea that these were "simple Christians" did not ring true. Kuznetsov was a controlling and irrational leader. He demanded that his followers must eat the right food, nothing processed; that they must not watch television; they must not handle any money; that barcodes on shopping items were evil, containing satanic messages, as were national ID cards and passports that contained the numbers 666, the latter of which he ordered his followers to burn.

At this point, Kuznetsov ordered that a cave be built in a snow-covered hillside, in which his followers should take refuge. There they would be safe; there they would wait for the end of the world to come in May 2008, and should anyone try to get them out, they would threaten mass suicide. In early November 2007, nearly thirty adults and four children (including a sixteen-month-old infant) went into the cave. Kuznetsov, stating that for now God had other things for him to do, remained in the village.

Kuznetsov spoke to the press from behind the door of his home in the small village of Nikolskoye.

A CULT EMERGES

When news broke of the small community living in dangerous circumstances with children (the sect had taken gas canisters and kerosene with them), the Russian authorities tried to persuade them to leave the cave, but the group assured them that they were warm, safe, and should be left alone. Having covered the cave entrance, the group insisted the police leave, going on to threaten that they would blow up the gas tank they had with them should any further action be taken.

The police took Kuznetsov in for questioning. "He said his followers should not be disturbed, that they are the chosen ones, and that no one else is allowed to get in the cave," an officer told the press. Relatives from as far away as Belarus and Ukraine came to the scene, trying to persuade loved ones to come out, but they were greeted with a vow of silence, and it was only when heavy snow—four months after their submergence—caused a wall to collapse that fourteen members walked out. They were followed by nine more who needed medical attention.

Time was ticking and as Kuznetsov's predicted doomsday date came, his own mental health was questioned (police had found him sleeping in a coffin), and fearing that he may commit suicide, he was taken into hospital. In mid-May 2008, the remaining followers came out. They were suffering from the toxic fumes produced by the decomposing bodies of two followers who had died in the cave over the winter. Having removed the dead bodies, the authorities blew up the cave.

Kuznetsov was taken into care, and in time was diagnosed with paranoia and a chronic mental disorder. While he remained in hospital receiving treatment the cult broke up, with many returning to their homes. It was said that one family continued to live in the village, without electricity or passports, awaiting the end of the world.

Erzhey village houses the center of the Kaa-Khem Old Believers in Tuva, Siberia.

CASE NOTES: THE OLD BELIEVERS

In the seventeenth century, the Russian Orthodox Church was subject to a number of ritual and textual revisions by the Patriarch Nikon of Moscow, who felt the church had wrongly deviated from its Greek origins and changes should be made. A group of conservative Russian Orthodox Christians broke from the church, angered by the reforms, and in protest renamed themselves "The Old Believers." Many of them, like Kuznetsov's cult, moved to remote communities.

4

CONSPIRACY
AND
NEW AGE

New Age philosophy is a collection
of spiritual and religious beliefs
that became popular in the
1970s, and along with conspiracy
theories, were incorporated into
the teachings of several cults.
The Nuwaubian Nation opened a
compound in Georgia, with Egyptian
pyramids and a huge Sphinx
statue, where its leader Dwight
York fathered nearly a hundred
children. Heaven's Gate promised
their followers that a spacecraft
would take their souls to heaven
if they first committed suicide
and exited their earthly bodies.

NXIVM

LOCATION:......... NEW YORK, USA; VANCOUVER, CANADA; MEXICO, SOUTH AMERICA

YEARS ACTIVE:.................... 1998-PRESENT DAY

FOUNDER:................................ KEITH RANIERE

They promised to change peoples' lives. Through secretive and expensive courses, members were promised that they would learn to unleash their inner perfection. By giving themselves completely over to the programs, paid-up members could overcome all the obstacles that were supposedly holding them back. They were promised that nothing was impossible if they were part of the group. But what was supposed to be self-help was causing physical and emotional harm. Who were NXIVM and how were they stopped?

NXIVM programs promised
unparalleled personal
and professional
development.

In 1998, Keith Raniere founded a new "Executive Success Program" (ESP) offering a range of techniques. NXIVM (pronounced *Nex-ee-um* and said to mean "the next millennium") promised its members greater self-fulfillment and success through a series of courses, by eliminating emotional barriers that had hitherto been blocking their progress.

Two years earlier, Raniere had been accused by the New York Attorney General of running a pyramid scheme, and while he denied any wrongdoing, he agreed to pay a $40,000 fine. Despite this background, Raniere's new venture was a success. Its many new members, paying thousands of dollars for their courses, would be asked to call him "Vanguard" (after a 1981 video game) and were told that their leader was a remarkable man. He claimed to have an IQ of 240, that he was a judo and track champion and an advanced piano player, and that he had multiple degrees (Raniere had graduated from polytechnic with a 2.26 GPA).

INITIAL SUCCESS

Raniere was a charming, manipulative man, and such was his charisma that by 2003, the company had grown rapidly, with 3,700 people taking part in its courses and programs. Clients included Hollywood actors, business leaders (allegedly including Richard Branson), and the heiresses to the Seagram empire, Clare and Sara Bronfman. The intensive five-day courses cost $2,700, and between 1998 and 2018, over 16,000 people across America, Canada, and Mexico signed up for them. Having completed the courses, lots of clients became more involved with NXIVM. There were incentives for further recruitment, and many who joined happily recounted having their anxieties and phobias removed, and some even suggested medical disorders such as Tourette's Syndrome and OCD were cured.

Prior to each session at the ESPs, a twelve-point mission statement was read out. Mantras such as "There are no ultimate victims; therefore, I will not choose to be a victim" were meant to uplift, but the courses also involved manipulative methods. Different-colored sashes were worn to denote rankings; hierarchies were practiced by standing when higher-ranking members walked into a room. The "Vanguard" himself was always greeted by a kiss on his mouth; long, seventeen-hour days were draining; and the emphasis was on obedience and subservience. High-ranking members would live together in communes, often not paid for their work instructing classes, and in time, spin-off classes exclusively for men or women offered further services at an additional cost.

SUSPICIONS AND ACCUSATIONS

In 2003, *Forbes Magazine* ran a story on NXIVM citing Raniere's supposed marketing fraud in the 1990s. Participants complained of both psychotic and hallucinogenic episodes after ESP sessions, and the article went on to state that "Detractors say he runs a cult-like program aimed at breaking down his subjects psychologically, separating them from their families and inducting them into a bizarre world of messianic pretensions, idiosyncratic language, and ritualistic practices."

Despite the report and the use of the term "cult," the group continued to attract great interest and support. But, while it prospered, whispers of worrying irregularities and accounts of unethical and unlawful practices were never far away. In 2012, Albany's *Times Union* newspaper published a story that accused Raniere of sexual and even child abuse. No charges were ever brought.

In 2017, *The New York Times* ran an interview with a high-ranking member who had been physically abused. At this point, the truth began to come out. Sarah Edmondson had joined NXIVM in 2005. Enthused by the group and a prolific recruiter, Edmondson was based in Vancouver and became active with the women-only subsidiary called D.O.S. (Dominus Obsequious Sororium – "master over the slave women"). In the article, Edmondson spoke graphically about how the group's "master," Lauren Salzman, had in March 2017 forced her into an initiation that involved her being branded using a cauterizing pen. To join D.O.S., Edmondson had been asked to provide nude photos, damaging information about herself, and information about her loved ones. The group had a motto, "Collateralize Your Life," meaning that by giving such information, members were pledging themselves forever.

Punishments for perceived wrongdoings such as not answering a text within a minute included being starved and stripped naked and paddled with a sado-masochistic instrument. Often these punishments would be videoed and sent to Raniere.

Edmondson was told to have a tattoo and while skeptical, she agreed, but on arrival at a high-ranking member's house, she was horrified to discover that she and other new recruits would, in fact, be blindfolded, held down on a medical table, and branded on their pelvic area. Having been made to say, "Master, please brand me, it would be an honor," the women suffered their skin being seared for forty-five agonizing minutes. Having endured extreme pain, Edmondson described her horror on discovering that the symbol branded onto her skin actually included the letters "KR"—Keith Raniere's initials. Another member told of being forced to watch videos of Mexican cartel members decapitating women and children, in what was called "a fright experiment." Edmondson's account in *The New York Times* became big news, providing more accounts of systematic abuse within the cult, and many members left. In February 2018, a complaint was issued in federal court, and the hunt for Raniere was on.

ARREST AND IMPRISONMENT

Keith Raniere had fled to Mexico, but officers there soon found him. He was arrested and deported back to New York. Charges against him included sex trafficking, forced labor, and possession of child pornography. Other members such as Salzman and the actress Allison Mack (see Case Notes, opposite) were also indicted on various charges, including identity theft, extortion, forced labor, sex trafficking, money laundering, wire fraud, and obstruction of justice. The women who had worked with Raniere initially denied the charges but soon pleaded guilty to lesser indictments, in lieu of not standing trial.

So, Raniere stood trial alone. In June 2019, he was found guilty of numerous charges and in October 2020 was sentenced to 120 years in prison. Today, despite launching unsuccessful appeals, he is serving his sentence in a maximum-security penitentiary in Arizona, designated for sex offenders. From there he is said to still regard himself as the head of NXIVM, communicating with his dwindling membership by email. In the summer of 2020, a number of supporters arrived at his jail (then in Brooklyn) for a vigil and to dance and show their support. Prison officers moved Raniere so he couldn't see them. Raniere communicated to the followers that to get him moved back to his old cell, they should endear themselves to the officers by bringing them coffee and donuts.

Mack was a well-known actor before becoming an active participant in NXVIM's murky activities.

CASE NOTES: ALLISON MACK

Keith Raniere and his NXIVM group had many loyal followers. Among them was the actor Allison Mack. Mack was famous for her role in the television series *Smallville*, and became active with the Vancouver chapter of the cult, getting further involved with the master/slave "D.O.S." subsidiary. Mack was a "first-line master" and they would tell recruits that as an all-women group, Raniere had nothing to do with their work. The truth was, he was very much involved and would receive photos and videos of members and initiations.

When Sarah Edmondson went to *The New York Times* with her horrific account of being branded by the group, not only did the symbol include the initials "KR," but also, underlining the importance of Mack to Raniere's group, the initials "AM" were visible. Mack recruited many women who were forced into sexual activity with Raniere, but due to her cooperation and evidence, in June 2021, she was sentenced to just three years in jail.

AETHERIUS
SOCIETY

LOCATION:.............................. LONDON, UK, AND
LOS ANGELES, USA

YEARS ACTIVE:.................... 1954-PRESENT DAY

FOUNDER:...................................... GEORGE KING

They come in peace. Throughout the history of mankind, religious figures from Buddha to Jesus, from Krishna to Lao Tzu have come to Earth as extra-terrestrial beings to lead the human race to a more enlightened future. One man in the 1950s claimed to experience contact with these beings and, believing himself to be a conduit through which aliens could communicate, he created a new movement—a movement he and his followers believe will advance humans into a new and better age.

In the mid-1950s, the joy and optimism that the Western world experienced after defeating the Nazis a decade earlier had largely been replaced by new fears. The Cold War had cast its frosty shadow from Moscow to Washington as a new, seemingly unprecedented danger loomed over the human race.

It was in these unsure times that a former taxi driver in his small London flat in 1954 had his first poignant contact with the unearthly beings who he felt would help him to change the world. "Prepare yourself! You are to become the voice of Interplanetary Parliament," were the words that came to him, he says, "with a somewhat gentle firmness."

George King had devoted much of his life to yoga, and through the extreme practice of it, not merely as a form of exercise or mindfulness, he claimed to have developed instinctive powers that made him fully aware that this had not been some sort of trick of the mind. When these powers also allowed for the visitation of an Indian yoga master, King was given detailed instructions on what was to be done. From here on, King was the "Primary Terrestrial Mental Channel" and the Aetherius Society was born.

King claimed to have been visited by Krishna, among many other religious figures.

COSMIC MASTERS

King's beliefs, which continue to be taught by his Society to this day, center around the notion that these figures would come to Earth to teach the right way, and how to use their technology and spirituality, so far advanced compared with our own as to be undetectable by our scientific methods. So, Krishna came from Saturn, the home of the "Cosmic Hierarchy." Jesus and Buddha both came from Venus and they, like Moses and Confucius, came to us through George King, to teach us true spirituality while also performing other metaphysical acts that according to the Society's website were "vital to the survival of our civilization on this planet." These visitors were called the "Cosmic Masters" by King and the Aetherius Society, and they would come to the group's founder, who, by entering a state of meditation known as *Samadhi,* would communicate and receive the messages that they sent.

It was on a holy hill in North Devon, England, that King once encountered "Master Jesus." King described the meeting when the image of a man who had appeared from a spacecraft came to him. "Dimly out of the corner of my eye I saw something in the sky. Then I saw a being which kind of appeared before me—I didn't see him walk up to me, I opened my eyes and he was there. He was very tall, he was dressed in a long robe, he had long brownish hair—there was so much radiance around the man. I knew, although he didn't tell me, I knew that he was Jesus and that he had come from the planet Venus—I didn't have to be told, I just knew this. I think it was some sort of telepathic impression that I picked up. There was no denying it and there was no denying his presence."

BELIEFS AND PRACTICES

While King has been able to see and communicate with these "religious" beings, he stated that they exist on a "spiritual level" and that by keeping a "higher vibratory rate" they have avoided detection from human space travel. King and the Society have always insisted that the intelligence he communicates with is from our own solar system. "I'm sure it would be easier for George to say he was communicating with intelligences from the other side of the Milky Way galaxy," an Aetherius priest called Alan Moseley told *The Washington Post* in 1997. "But you have to stick to the truth."

King practiced yoga, claiming to have developed the ability to communicate with cosmic figures.

By studying various Hindi and Vedic texts, and by referencing biblical symbols such as the Star of Bethlehem, the Society firmly believes that there have been clues to how extra-terrestrials have visited our planet and that they have been guiding humans for centuries.

Through the practice of yoga, prayer, and meditation, and their New Age beliefs in spiritual healing and alternative medicine, the Aetherius Society advocate environmental issues, are firmly anti-nuclear weapons, and believe that matters of climate change, like so many other societal troubles, are merely symptoms of a much larger spiritual problem. They also believe that through prayer and the redirection of spiritual energy, the human race can be saved.

To harness the power of prayer and redirect spiritual energy garnered from the Cosmic Masters, King himself secretly designed a "spiritual energy battery," a device he claimed could hold a "charge of spiritual energy for an indefinite period." By praying, chanting mantras, and focusing the energy into the battery, it can be stored and then released and manipulated to aid certain areas on the planet in need of help. King called this "Operation Prayer Power."

The Society believe that there are nineteen holy mountains on Earth, each imbued with cosmic significance by King, and that it is on these mountain tops, visited by pilgrims from the Society, such prayer and mantras are

The Aetherius Society
Health Foods store
in Fulham, southwest
London, in 1975.

conducted and particular global issues are dealt with. The Society's website explains it further when it says, "Have you always felt that there was more to life than the physical world we see around us? That there might be—must be—an all-pervasive, subtle energy that exists throughout the universe? To wise men and women throughout the ages, this energy isn't something vague or imaginary; it is something we can physically feel. They made themselves a channel for this energy, sent it outward for the spiritual healing and inspiration of others in need. They understood how they could invoke this energy through prayer. Not prayer in the sense of asking God for a favor, but in the yogic sense of radiating energy with true love."

ACHIEVEMENTS

The Aetherius Society has enjoyed great success with growing membership numbers in their two churches in London and Los Angeles. Even after

George King's death in 1997, the Society have continued to advocate their beliefs, remaining certain that through their leader's abilities and the power of their prayer, many problems that have befallen Earth have been solved.

A deadly hurricane heading for communities in the Caribbean in the 1990s was said to have "done a U-turn" out to sea, thanks to the Society's prayers. The war in Cyprus in 1974 owed its peaceful ending to the positivity of prayer, while the dangerous Russian nuclear disaster at Kyshtym in 1957 was said to be fixed by King and the Cosmic Masters. Paul Nugent, a priest in the Society, told huckmag. com in 2018 that "beings from other worlds had a very active role in cleaning that up." More recently, the tensions between North Korea, their southern neighbors, and the USA have been prayed for by the Society, as have the situation in Ukraine and conflicts in Africa, with what the Society claim are positive results.

CASE NOTES: THE SILENCE GROUP

George King and his Society have long argued that the information and communication that was afforded to him has also been relayed to global governments, but a group of individuals called "The Silence Group" have suppressed the messages. Instead, these powerful people in the world of finance and politics have been able to keep the public misinformed and run the planet on their terms.

About the group, King once said, "Dear friends, do not let the conspirators be successful. It does exist. The Silence Group—what is it? I will tell you beyond all doubt. It is run by the great financial organizations—organizations that move countries—organizations which cause conflict between one country and another, so that war may result. So that their profit may be great indeed."

NUWAUBIAN NATION

LOCATION:......... NEW YORK AND GEORGIA, USA

YEARS ACTIVE:.................................. 1967-2004

FOUNDER:.................................... DWIGHT YORK

The Black separatist Dwight York preached messages taken from a wide array of ideologies and religions, anything from ancient Egyptian to New Age philosophies, while behind the scenes he conducted systematic sexual abuse at his remote compounds. Regularly changing his identity, York's followers believed that he was the new Messiah and allowed him to control every aspect of their lives.

In 1993, the locals in the picturesque, sparsely populated Putnam County, known as the "Dairy Capital of Georgia," were a little curious when York paid $1 million for 476 acres (2 square kilometers) of land. In the following years, York would build a compound featuring two 40-foot (12-meter) plywood and stucco Egyptian pyramids and a huge Sphinx statue, with rumors spreading that he had become a Native American chief, then wanted to be known as an alien.

Born in 1945, York was arrested for statutory rape in June 1964 for having sex with a 13-year-old girl. He was given a suspended sentence and probation, which he broke for being in possession of a deadly weapon, assault, and resisting arrest. He was jailed for three years.

On his release, York roamed the New York streets, selling incense and pamphlets extolling his views on Islam and Black nationalism. He began calling himself "Imaam Isa Abdullah" and from 1967 built up some followers, who he formed into a group known as Ansar Pure Sufi. In the early 1970s, he moved from Harlem to Brooklyn, where his followers were renamed the Ansaru Allah Community (AAC) and asked to dress in black and green dashikis. He changed his name again to Dr. Malachi Z. York.

Over the next decade, the group rapidly expanded to around 500 followers, living in the Bushwick area of Brooklyn. They owned bookstores, a clothing store, and a grocery store. The group opened more branches across the country, including in Atlanta, Detroit, Philadelphia, and Baltimore, and abroad in London, Toronto, Trinidad, and Jamaica.

The Egyptian-themed Tama-Re compound was built by the Nuwaubian Nation in 1993 in Putnam County, Georgia.

"I THOUGHT HE WAS THE MESSIAH"

In Brooklyn, York's followers were told to surrender all possessions and work for free, selling pamphlets on the street, and if they did not make $100 each day they were beaten by other followers and eventually thrown out. York asserted control over all aspects of his followers' lives: he chose their partners and they had to ask his permission if they wanted to have sex with each other. York wrote 450 booklets called "scrolls" to promote his teachings, and during the 1980s launched a brief music career, performing with groups Jackie and the Starlights, the Students, and Passion. Under the artist name Dr. York, he recorded and released music on his own record label, Passion Productions.

"Malachi York has a lot of charisma," said Robert Rohan, a committed follower for sixteen years. "There are people in life you meet who can draw you in with their conversation. That was him. My first thought was 'Wow, a Black Jesus' when I saw the picture of him inside the books he wrote . . . It gave me a sense of Black pride."

In 1983, York relocated some of the group to a large property he called Camp Jazzir Abba in the Catskills mountains in upstate New York. By then he had an estimated 3,000 followers, many of whom lived there in trailers, while he lived in luxury in a mansion. He increasingly began to take advantage of his followers, and speculation spread that there was also sexual abuse.

RURAL GEORGIA

In 1993, York bought a property in Putnam County and eventually moved most of his followers there, telling them this was their chance to meet their "spiritual parents." In reality, he needed to flee from New York as the FBI were beginning to investigate his activities. He demanded to be called "Chief Black Thunderbird Eagle," then told his followers he was an alien from the Planet Rizq.

York declared that their new compound, which would become known as "Tama-Re," would be sovereign land. "I'm talking about a real nation, our own nation," he said in a secret recording. "With our own passports, with our own tax system, where no one tells us what to do but us."

In fact, York used the seclusion of the compound to sexually abuse children as young as four years old. "He would allow the children to watch cartoons and feed them ice cream," said Tracey Bowen, a lieutenant in the Putnam County Sheriff's Office. "It was a progression, a complete grooming process he did with these kids."

Former follower Niki Lopez spoke about how she joined York's group as an 11-year-old with her mother, and the grooming began when she was 13. "He would give us little treats," she said. She was taught how to perform oral sex by one of York's wives, then at 15 she was held down and raped by him.

By 1998, York's regime of abuse was becoming harder to conceal when the local sheriff Howard Sills began to hear about huge numbers of underage girls giving birth in local hospitals. "The girls weren't allowed to speak," he said. "All the speaking had to be done through the men, and they would take the placenta with them when they left. I suspected it was from keeping us from matching DNA to York."

The United Nuwaubian Nation Of Moors' Religious Compound In Eatonton, Georgia.

The sheriff began to receive anonymous letters informing him York was molesting children. In 2001, York's estranged son Jacob told the authorities his father was sexually abusing children and helped them build their case against him. The sheriff visited the compound, where he was greeted by guards on the entrance holding machine guns. He wanted to close "Club Ramses," a nightclub within the compound which they believed posed a severe fire hazard. York and his followers responded by branding Sills "a race-hater of Blacks" and a member of the Ku Klux Klan, and printed a publication with the headline: "The Whites in Putnam County Hate Blacks."

"I pulled back," Sills said. "Normally, I'd never do that. But they clearly were desperate for an armed confrontation, and I was not going to give it." Instead, by the spring of 2002 the FBI had interviewed thirty-five alleged victims of York, and believed he had fathered around ninety-five children, though the real figure could have been as high as 300. They now had more than enough evidence to take action.

RAID ON THE COMPOUND

On May 8, 2002, nearly 300 federal and state law enforcement officers waited until York and his "main wife" Kathy Johnson had driven out of the compound before they arrested them at a local grocery store. With the couple in custody, officers entered the compound, where they encountered up to a hundred followers but met no resistance. There they found a stockpile of weapons, a Pink Panther plush toy with a penis attached, and a "census" book with names, pictures, and birthdates for nearly a hundred of what they believed were York's children.

In April 2004, York was sentenced to 135 years in prison after being found guilty of four counts of racketeering and six child molestation-related charges, including transporting minors across state lines for sexual purposes. His appeals were rejected, and he is currently serving his sentence at a maximum-security prison in Florence, Colorado.

"I classify him as an indiscriminate sexual predator," said former FBI agent Jalaine Ward, who investigated him. "His power and money along with his demented personality created this monster."

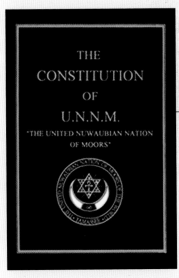

THE
CONSTITUTION
OF
U.N.N.M.
"THE UNITED NUWAUBIAN NATION
OF MOORS"

York set out
his beliefs for
his followers
in a written
constitution
published in 1993.

CASE NOTES:
WHAT DID THE NUWAUBIANS BELIEVE?

It is difficult to grasp exactly what York preached to his followers as it constantly changed, but it was a febrile mixture of Islam, Black nationalism, Christianity, Judaism, New Age philosophy, UFO religions, and Egyptology.

The Southern Poverty Law Center has stated: "Nuwaubian mythology is a disorienting mix of UFO theories, talk about the significance of Egypt and the pyramids, references to Atlantis, and retellings of stories from the Bible and other religious texts."

However, the one message of York's that never changed was that Blacks were the original humans and superior to other races. "White people are the devil. They say the Nuwaubians are not racist, bullcrap! I am . . . White people are devils, always was, always will be," he once said in a lecture.

THE

FAMILY

LOCATION:............FERNY CREEK, VICTORIA,
AUSTRALIA

YEARS ACTIVE:...................................1964-93

FOUNDER:.....................ANNE HAMILTON-BYRNE

In 1987, a troubled teenage girl was introduced to two policemen by a
private detective. What the girl said about her upbringing would shock
the most hardened officers. When her voice was joined by those of
other children from the same community, the lid was lifted on a truly
vile and dangerous cult. Its charismatic but abusive leader escaped
justice until her death in 2019, despite the cruelty she presided over
in a cult simply known as The Family.

Members of The Family were experimenting with the hallucinogenic drug LSD.

Born in 1921, Anne Hamilton-Byrne grew up in Sale, around two hours' drive east of Melbourne, Australia, and lived a troubled childhood. Her mother, from London, UK, was diagnosed with paranoid schizophrenia and spent over two decades in an asylum. Hamilton-Byrne married her first husband aged just 20, with whom she had a child, but her husband was killed in a car crash in 1955. Hamilton-Byrne was said to have had numerous miscarriages and the couple had been looking into adopting more children. In the early 1960s, she began to teach yoga and soon had a budding practice attracting mainly middle-aged, middle-class women and gay men. The women, often in unhappy marriages, were looking for new lives; gay men were seeking solace from Australia's still strict laws against homosexuality.

THE FAMILY GROWS

It was a meeting with Dr. Raynor Johnson, an eminent but soon to be retired physicist at the University of Melbourne, that sparked the start of the group's ascent. Dr. Johnson was himself fascinated by the ever-popular topic of spiritualism and his meetings with Hamilton-Byrne convinced him that she possessed extrasensory perception (ESP). Together with some other members of the group, Hamilton-Byrne and Dr. Johnson experimented with LSD, and in the "name of research" he began to be increasingly convinced that she was indeed divine, claiming eventually that she was the Messiah, or Jesus reborn. In his diary he wrote that she was, "Unquestionably the wisest, the serenest, and most gracious and generous soul I have ever met."

Dr. Johnson and his wife purchased a house in Ferny Creek, a small hamlet on the outskirts of Melbourne, where Hamilton-Byrne now lived. Attracted by Johnson's reputation, middle-class professionals came to attend sermons and meditation sessions held at a lodge the group had built with donations from followers. They called their group The Great-White Brotherhood, but soon it would be simply known as The Family.

The group's main belief was that Hamilton-Byrne was the reincarnation of Jesus and the senior members were her apostles, but that didn't mean they were exclusively preaching Christian beliefs. Their message was instead a mix of Christianity, Hinduism, and teachings from fashionable Eastern gurus. They believed that like Jesus, Buddha and Krishna had come to Earth to enlighten humanity, and that Hamilton-Byrne was the latest in this line of living gods.

Donations came in, new meeting halls and properties were built or purchased, and members moved into homes in the surrounding area. LSD became a major factor in the sessions, but a family is not a family without children, and from the beginning of the 1970s, they began to appear with worrying regularity.

KAI LAMA

Some of them were the children of members, some were "adopted" from vulnerable teenage mothers, and all were unknowingly forced into Hamilton-Byrne's world, given her name, and made to live under her rules. Using her vast membership contacts and relying on how stigmatized unmarried mothers were at that time in Australia, Hamilton-Byrne was able to use doctors, nurses, and lawyers to find the children for her, and to have false documents drawn up. Each child was told that she was their mother, she would wear homemade loose dresses when faking pregnancies, and spoke of how her children would survive the end of the world and become the new master race.

A new property they called Kai Lama was used to house the children, where they were kept in seclusion, home-schooled, and looked after mainly by other members, known as "aunties" and "uncles." Hamilton-Byrne and her new husband Bill lived in a separate home nearby.

Anne Hamilton-Byrne claimed to be the reincarnation of Christ.

The children (there were up to fourteen by 1975) had hardly any contact with the outside world, but those who did see them would have noticed that not only were they all dressed the same, but that the majority of them had their hair bleached white blonde, perhaps a symbol of the master race Hamilton-Byrne had spoken of.

THE TRUTH COMES OUT

In 1987, at the age of 17, one of Hamilton-Byrne's "daughters," Sarah, was told to leave the group. To its members, living in fear of the outside world, this was the ultimate punishment. Sarah had become argumentative and assertive, and having contacted a private detective who had her suspicions about what was happening at Kai Lama, she was introduced to two police officers. As a result of her statement, the police raided the property in August that year.

Sarah learned through the private detective that Hamilton-Byrne was not her biological mother and that she and so many of her "siblings" had been adopted. The other children at Kai Lama were taken into care, and it was through their descriptions of life there that police learned the truth. Hamilton-Byrne had abused the children emotionally and physically. She had lied to them about their parentage but also told them that she was of European royal descent and owned castles. In time, they had grown to both adore and worship her.

Hamilton-Byrne gave the everyday parenting role to various "aunties," female members, themselves intimidated by their leader. The aunties would carry out beatings, lock the children away for days (there was a secret corridor that led to a hiding place under the house, in case of visitors), deny them food, and when they suspected a child had done wrong, the aunties would dunk the child's head in a bucket of water until the child confessed. Valium was used to keep the children docile, and then, at the age of 14, they would be forced to take LSD in a ritual called "going through." Many children went on to suffer long-term psychological effects.

Hamilton-Byrne herself would inflict beatings, often using a stiletto shoe, but despite the cruelty, the children were more than loyal, transfixed by her imposing character and her sermons, and convinced by the idea that she was so much more than their mother. In one police interview after the raid in 1987, a teenage child said, "It's hard to say how devoted we were to her; how we hung off her every look and every thought she had about us. We wanted so much for her to love us, but I don't think she ever really did."

NO JUSTICE

Such was the wealth amassed by Hamilton-Byrne (police estimated it to be almost $50 million but many felt it was far more), she and her husband were able to flee, before finally being arrested in their property in Catskills, USA, in 1993 and extradited back to Australia. No firm legal charges of abuse could be made, and the charges of perjury and conspiracy to defraud were dropped. Only on the charge of making a false declaration (involving the children's birth certificates) were she and her husband found guilty. Each was fined $5,000. While some members sued Hamilton-Byrne with successful results, she continued to deny any wrongdoing. In 2016, while making a documentary about The Family, filmmaker Rosie Jones met her in a Melbourne nursing home. Suffering from dementia, Hamilton-Byrne could not be interviewed. "Her speech was mostly incoherent," said Jones, "but she sat there nursing a plastic baby doll."

Sarah Moore was instrumental in lifting the lid on The Family's activities.

CASE NOTES: SARAH MOORE

Many of the children brought into The Family suffered post-traumatic stress disorder (PTSD), and some even took their own lives. Sarah Moore (her real name) herself attempted suicide, but despite the trauma, she went on to have a relationship with her biological mother and write a book, *Unseen, Unheard, Unknown*. Having studied medicine she became a doctor, practicing in both the Melbourne area and South Asia, where she volunteered to help children in India and Thailand. Moore continued to suffer with bipolar disorder and PTSD. In 2016, she died of heart failure.

THE

BRETHREN

LOCATION:..USA

YEARS ACTIVE:.................... 1971-PRESENT DAY

FOUNDER:.............................. JIMMIE ROBERTS

Some were athletic, others were Grade-A students, most were at universities, and many had their own religious beliefs, but one by one, they were disappearing. As parents all over America feared for the whereabouts of their children, it became clear that they had fallen in with a strange, enigmatic man, whose followers called him "The Elder." They had fallen in with The Brethren.

The son of a part-time Pentecostal preacher, Jimmie Roberts was a mediocre student. He spent time with the Marine Corps before running a hairdressing salon, but all the while he was developing his own extreme views of the world and religion. By the end of the 1960s, he was adamant that these were "the end of days," that mainstream churches were too worldly and too corrupt to meet the needs of God's true believers. In 1971, he created his own sect called The Brethren.

Roberts started by recruiting followers in California and Colorado, promoting the giving up of possessions, of material belongings, technology, and finances. Roberts was a charismatic figure who would focus on the infiltration of young adults in small towns and college campuses across the country. Such were his mesmerizing eyes, enigmatic leadership qualities (forged from his time in the Marines), and his air of authority that soon dozens of young people had completely relinquished their material goods and dropped out of jobs, college courses, and society in general.

THE BROTHERHOOD

Throughout the 1970s, Roberts' brotherhood grew rapidly. Small cells appeared across the country, with young adults, once-successful students with loving families of their own, now seen in towns and cities all over America living like vagrants. They would rummage through bins, giving the cult the nickname "The Garbage-Eaters."

Roberts, an elusive leader, continued to preach that the end of the world was soon to be upon them, and that only his followers, with their lifestyles purified, could be saved. The Brethren's doctrines took the passages of the Bible very literally. Roberts insisted that his followers should dress like Jesus and his disciples, so men wore long tunics and grew beards; the women wore long skirts, baggy shirts, and never wore any makeup.

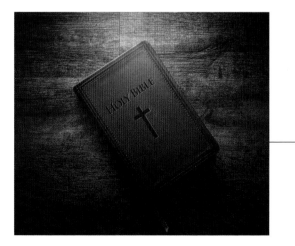

Cult leader Jimmie Roberts took passages of the Bible literally.

The group was broken up into cells, but only Roberts would have knowledge of where each cell was located. Converts were indoctrinated into believing the world was soon to end, that their salvation lay solely in immediate obedience, and that should they show pure loyalty to the group, they could learn to be like Jesus himself. This included the dropping of all materialism, nor could there be any laughing or dancing, and once converted, there was to be no contact with outside family members, including parents.

The individual cells would be forced to live nomadic lifestyles for fear of detection by police and searching parents, and no work could ever be taken on full-time. Food must be foraged for from behind grocery stores and restaurants, and they must travel only using bicycles or by hitchhiking. The leader would live in the same way, staying in the same camps, eating the same discarded food, and wear the same austere clothes. He could, however, use commercial transport.

One of the most controversial doctrines that these followers had to live by was the prohibition of medicines. Roberts argued that doctors and medicine were examples of a lack of faith and so any ailments, from minor dental issues to the alleged case of a member left to die from pneumonia, were to be managed without medical care.

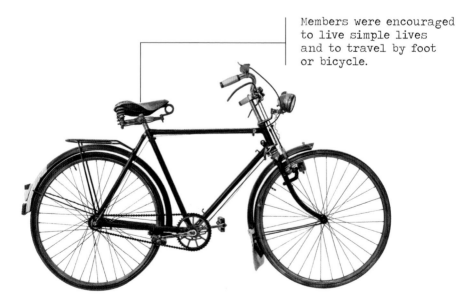

Members were encouraged to live simple lives and to travel by foot or bicycle.

THE CULT TODAY

Into the 1980s and 1990s, reports surrounding The Brethren were universally negative. Parent groups used media platforms to discuss Roberts and his brotherhood, and such was the sense that these young people had been taken from their families and their lives, almost against their will, that Roberts became increasingly elusive. In 1998, reports that members were being taken from their cells by force further fueled fears.

In February 2016, Jimmie Roberts died. It was thought he had suffered from cancer. He had not sought any medical help. During his lifetime, Roberts never saw his group number over a hundred core members. His Brethren group survives today and is headed by Jerry Williams, who in November 2022 talked to the *Denver Post*, saying, "We require what the Messiah required—it has to do with forsaking worldly possessions and living for God every day."

CASE NOTES: THE ROBERTS GROUP PARENTS NETWORK

With scores of young adults dropping out of society and joining The Brethren over the years, similar numbers of parents have been left heartbroken. Families have been ripped apart, and while some have managed to make contact, either by letter or in person, for many it has simply meant the loss of a child. The Roberts Group Parents Network is a support network for parents trying to locate their children. "We've been brought together from all parts of the country by our common loss," they write on their website. "Our sorrow is the same. In supporting each other we find new strength to make it through one day at a time and the new hope that we'll be reunited with the loved ones that were taken from our lives."

LOVE
HAS WON

LOCATION:.............CRESTONE, COLORADO, USA

YEARS ACTIVE:...................2006-PRESENT DAY

FOUNDER:....................................AMY CARLSON

In April 2021, a man walked into a police department and told officers that should they visit his house, they would find the mummified remains of Amy Carlson. An investigation followed into the death of Carlson, the apparent "Mother God" of a group called "Love Has Won." Police found her corpse enshrined, wrapped in a sleeping bag, decorated in Christmas lights, with her eyeless sockets sprinkled with glitter. What had led to this bizarre discovery?

Amy Carlson was born on the outskirts of Wichita in Kansas. The eldest of three sisters, her parents separated when she was a child and she divided her time between her mother in Oklahoma and her father in Kansas. They both remarried and she suffered difficult family relationships, especially with her stepmother.

As a child, Carlson became spiritual and told her parents that she could speak to angels. Archeia Faith, a former member of the group, told *Rolling Stone* magazine that Carlson had spoken to them of a time when she interrupted a sermon. "The pastor said something that she knew was a lie, since she was Jesus, and she yelled 'You're lying!' and had to be removed from church."

Carlson relocated to Dallas and later Houston. A popular and "charming" girl, by her early twenties, she had been married, divorced, and had three children. Her family claimed that she lacked any maternal instincts and that the children were frequently left with other people.

By now, Carlson's New Age beliefs were dominating her life. In the mid-2000s, she posted regularly on a New Age website called lightworkers.org and chatted to a man called Amerith WhiteEagle in Crestone, Colorado, who suggested to her that she was divine. In time she maintained that she could and did experience otherworldly, paranormal phenomena. On September 1, 2007, Carlson posted a claim that she had heard a melodic voice in her kitchen, telling her that she would be President of the United States.

WhiteEagle continued to convince Carlson that she was the "Mother God" to his "Father God," and very soon she left her job managing a McDonald's, left her children, and in a post written in December 2007, told her readers that she had released her "3-D relationship" and was moving to be with her "Mountain Man in Colorado."

Crestone was a place awash with New Agers, spiritualists, and ufologists, and the posts

The small town of Crestone is home to the mysterious Ziggurat, a place for private prayer and meditation.

loaded on YouTube (the group's initial name was "Galactic Federation of Light") told viewers that they too could be loved unconditionally and that they were to look within themselves for their own divine likeness. In 2009, the group posted under the name Love Has Won and soon they were posting content almost daily.

CLAIMS AND BELIEFS

At first, Carlson and WhiteEagle's posts were simple New Age teachings they had found elsewhere online, such as suggestions like that of the Ashtar Command, an extra-terrestrial agency that would enforce its law and one day save humanity.

It wasn't until Carlson and WhiteEagle's relationship ended (he left in 2014) that the group's messages became much more radical. She would talk about her own divinity; that she was, in fact, a 19-billion-year-old deity, that she was God, that she had been reincarnated hundreds of times over the years

Carlson believed in many conspiracy theories, including those of QAnon.

and had lived the lives of, among others, Jesus, Joan of Arc, Cleopatra, and Marilyn Monroe.

Carlson stated that Donald Trump had been her father in their past lives, and that the deceased spirit of the actor Robin Williams was able to communicate with her. Carlson and the group also discussed conspiracy theories, many suggested by QAnon, claiming that reptilian forces ran the world, that the planet was being forced to run on "low vibrations," and that she had been placed on Earth to help guide it into a higher state of being.

In 2014, Miguel Lamboy joined Love Has Won, and soon the group had up to twenty core members living with Carlson in Crestone. Every day they would post on their website and YouTube. Here they would teach their beliefs, recruit new members, and, crucially, they would sell vitamins and solicit donations with which to fund their lives. Lamboy declared that when he joined, he was suffering with terminal lung cancer, but he had been healed by the "Mother God" Carlson and he was now a true believer. He was also a useful asset financially. The group offered to heal illnesses and would charge $88 per session for "etheric surgery." Lamboy was organized and good with finances, and with his quiet guidance, the group gained non-profit charitable status in 2019.

AN ABUSIVE GROUP

With Lamboy's input and growing online membership, all seemed well in the movement. Believing in Carlson's celestial body and their desire to orbit around it, members viewed her posted videos in great numbers. Charming, positive, and charismatic, Carlson was popular. Her messages, however outlandish to some, were reaching people—but all was not as it seemed. The local police authorities had been asked to investigate allegations of fraud, and that followers had left their families having been "brainwashed" by Carlson. In 2020, a member was found wandering in the Colorado wilderness, naked, dehydrated, and disoriented. The member had been told by the group that he was "on the wrong side of the mountain" and that he lacked the "right energy."

Soon, other stories emerged from former members. Videos of apparent child cruelty alongside testaments around Carlson's drug and alcohol abuse spoke

Before her death, Carlson appeared on the popular television show *Dr. Phil*.

of a troubled and flawed leader. Carlson was said to be domineering and violent when she drank (witnesses suggested she drank vast amounts of vodka despite her ban of alcohol) and increasingly frequently she would appear on live streams in various states of inebriation.

In 2020, Carlson and two members of the group appeared on the *Dr. Phil* show, where they were accused of child cruelty and abuse, including racial and anti-Semitic slurs, which they fervently denied. It was, however, becoming clear that this was a troubled group, or cult, as many pundits and former members now called it.

It was a term that the group denied, but by the time of the *Dr. Phil* show, Carlson was drinking dangerous amounts. In 2018, a new member arrived. Jason Castillo had left his wife and kids to join the group, before becoming Carlson's "Earth Father." His behavior was erratic and violent, and he even broke another member's nose. With Carlson's drinking both frequent and heavy, the actual messages coming from the posted videos took on threatening tones, especially to those who didn't believe. "There's no fence sitting," said one member going by the name of El Moyra. "You either stand by Mother God or you'll be taken out."

THE LEADER DIES

By the autumn of 2020, Carlson's health was extremely frail. She had stated that she had cancer, and members, including Castillo, publicly suggested that her "earth body" was in danger. Members later reported that her legs no longer worked and that her skin was blue due to the overuse of colloidal silver, an ancient remedy used to treat infections (the group had been promoting it as a cure for Covid-19), and by the time the authorities came to the house after Lamboy had reported the presence of her body, it was thought that Carlson had died up to several weeks earlier. Later it transpired that Carlson had died in California and her body had been driven back to Colorado by her followers. A subsequent autopsy revealed that she had died from "alcohol abuse, anorexia, and chronic colloidal silver ingestion."

Upon Carlson's death, charges were raised against the group for child abuse, abuse of a corpse, and tampering with deceased human remains. The charges were eventually dropped. While many members left Love Has Won for other groups such as 5D Full Disclosure, and Castillo left to form another, smaller movement called "Joy Rains," Love Has Won continued to receive new members, sell products, and receive donations.

CASE NOTES: DISTURBING CLAIMS

When Amy Carlson was dying, shockingly, given her teachings about the outside "3-D World," she asked her members for medical intervention. Evidence suggests they refused. In a video posted in September 2021, a member said, "There have been moments when Mom has asked us to take her to a 3-D hospital and we're like 'Nope!' Because there's just, there's no way, and we know exactly how hijacking works," she said. "And, you can bet your f****** a** that someone in that hospital, whoever it would be, would get hijacked and go straight for Mom, try to do who knows what. They would try to take her to surgery. They would try to do some crazy s***. So, absolutely not."

HEAVEN'S GATE

LOCATION:............................ CALIFORNIA, USA

YEARS ACTIVE:.................................... 1975-97

FOUNDERS:...................MARSHALL APPLEWHITE
AND BONNIE NETTLES

Marshall Applewhite called his religious sect "the cult of cults," promising his followers a new life in heaven. When he teamed up with Bonnie Nettles, they claimed they were beings from another planet who had taken on human form, that they could help take others to heaven in a UFO, and that followers could achieve a "higher evolutionary level."

The cult was founded by Applewhite and Nettles after they met at a hospital in March 1972. Applewhite was there for heart surgery, and Nettles was his nurse. She told him he had been saved for a "special reason" and that they had a divine assignment.

Applewhite addresses his followers in a taped video message in 1997.

Born in Spur, Texas, in 1931, the son of a Presbyterian minister, Applewhite had been a soldier, an opera singer, and a music teacher before meeting 44-year-old Nettles. The pair did not have a romantic relationship, but found a common cause as both heard voices in their heads and believed they had "higher-level minds." Applewhite and Nettles also believed they were the two witnesses mentioned in the Book of Revelation, who spread a message of judgment but were martyred, resurrected, and taken to heaven in a cloud. They sought to recruit a band of followers, and in 1973 went on a spiritual road trip, which was largely unsuccessful. They were arrested for credit card fraud, but the charges were dropped. In August 1974, Applewhite served six months in a Missouri jail for stealing a rental car.

The duo began to use different names, including "Bo and Peep" and "Do and Ti," as they told people they were God's emissaries and could lead followers out of a corrupt world. By 1975, they had amassed around a hundred followers who accompanied them around the country. They took a trip to eastern Colorado, where their followers were told a spaceship would land in the desert and transport them to heaven, which ended in disappointment. The group moved to various campsites and compounds: Medicine Bow National Forest, Wyoming; Bonny Reservoir and Denver, Colorado; Salt Lake City, Utah; and Fort Worth, Texas. "The energy I felt from [Marshall] put me in a state of awe," said former follower Michael Conyers. "It told me he was a representative of the Kingdom of Heaven."

Followers had to abstain from alcohol, some foods, drugs, and sex. Applewhite and seven followers took some of this to an extreme, opting for surgical castration.

THE SPACECRAFT COMETH

In October 1996, the group moved into their final property in Rancho Santa Fe. They funded their operations through a side business called Higher Source, which built websites. "Sometimes it got pretty boring," said former follower Dick Joslyn. "Especially when you were waiting ten years for the spacecraft to come down." Applewhite possibly sensed his followers' frustration, so when he heard that the comet Hale Bopp was to become visible from Earth for the first time in 4,200 years, he told his followers this was a sign. A spacecraft following the comet would collect them. He told them to kill themselves so their souls could board the spacecraft. This was not suicide but the act of leaving their physical "vehicles" to progress to the "next level" above human, to be reincarnated in heaven.

On March 20, 1997, Applewhite and his followers began to record their farewell messages. From March 22, they commenced the suicides in three shifts over three days, when followers took a lethal dose of phenobarbital mixed with apple sauce and vodka, before placing a plastic bag over their heads to suffocate. The cult had sent their farewell videos and letters to a

Thirty-nine bodies were found at this mansion in Rancho Sante Fe in March 1997.

collection of people and organizations, stating they had "exited our vehicles." This included to fellow follower Rio DiAngelo, who went to the mansion and first discovered their bodies. On the afternoon of March 26, 1997, the San Diego County Sheriff's Department received an anonymous call (from DiAngelo) telling them there had been "a mass suicide" at a mansion in Rancho Santa Fe. On arrival Deputy Robert Brunk knew immediately it had not been a crank call. "I noticed an odor that in my past experience has been associated with death," Brunk said.

Inside the mansion, police found thirty-nine decomposing bodies— twenty-one women and eighteen men—who had apparently all committed suicide. They were found lying face-up on mattresses; most had purple shrouds placed over them. All were wearing black sweatsuits, and a brand-new pair of black and white Nike sneakers. The upper arm on each of their sweatshirts featured a badge that said, "Heaven's Gate Away Team." In each of their pockets was a $5 bill and three quarters. Applewhite was found dead in the main bedroom.

CASE NOTES: APPLEWHITE'S COMPOUND RULES

"Most cults want to sweet-talk, draw you in and make you feel love. These guys weren't like that," said former follower Joan Culpepper. Instead Applewhite enforced strict rules and discipline within his compounds. His followers were allowed only six minutes to use the bathroom each day, they underwent enemas, and had to dress in baggy clothes and have short haircuts. They were allowed to leave the compound but had to sign out to be given their driver's license and car keys. There was "tomb time" when they were not allowed to speak to each other for days, and they had tuning forks taped on their heads to erase human thoughts.

"It was like the military," says Dick Joslyn, who was a follower for fifteen years. "There were all these procedures that drove some people crazy."

5

ECCENTRIC AND WEIRD

Most cults promote some weird
practices, but the ones featured
here took them to new levels.
Members of Synanon, whose leader
Charles Dederich even admitted
"I am considered a megalomaniac
nut," attempted to murder one of
their critics with a rattlesnake.
Meanwhile, Universal Medicine
in Australia suggested to their
followers that they burp loudly
to rid their bodies of any evil
spirits; and the inhabitants of
a South Pacific island worshipped
the UK's Prince Philip.

THE
PRINCE PHILIP
MOVEMENT

LOCATION:............................ TANNA, VANUATA,
                                     SOUTH PACIFIC

YEARS ACTIVE:.................. 1960S-PRESENT DAY

FOUNDER:.. UNKNOWN

The island of Tanna, in the island country of Vanuatu, deep in
the South Pacific, is 25 miles (40 kilometers) long and 12 miles
(20 kilometers) wide. It has a population of 29,000 and has been
inhabited from around 400 BCE. In August 1774, Captain James
Cook arrived. Drawn by the inflamed summit of the volcano, Mount
Yasur, Cook was the first European on the island, but over the years,
many visitors from other cultures, including whalers, traders, and
missionaries, followed in his footsteps. The most notable visitor of
all, though—at least to some tribespeople—was the late Prince Philip,
Duke of Edinburgh and husband of the late Queen Elizabeth II, who to
them was not just a member of the royal family but also a divine being.

The beautiful South Pacific island of Tanna, once home to the Prince Philip Movement.

In 1974, the nation of Tanna was proclaimed independent from British–French rule. Since then, apart from interruptions by cyclones and droughts, the island has continued in a fairly peaceful way, with its population almost entirely made up of Indigenous Melanesians who have lived their lives in a similar fashion to their ancient ancestors.

In the village of Yaohnanen, a prophecy passed down through the ages spoke of a mountain spirit that traveled over the island and that one day that spirit's son, taking the form of a pale-faced man, would leave their volcano, travel to a far, foreign land, marry a powerful lady, and at some point return to them. In the 1960s, having seen the respect that both the Queen and Prince Philip were afforded by colonial officials, the villagers concluded that Philip must be the man, the god, that had been prophesied in the legend.

A ROYAL VISIT

In 1974, Queen Elizabeth II and Prince Philip visited the South Pacific aboard the Royal Yacht *Britannia*, including a stop at Tanna. Chief of the village and respected warrior Jack Naiva went out to sea to greet the yacht and saw the Prince, later saying, "I saw him standing on the deck in his white uniform. I knew then that he was the true messiah."

Prince Philip was unaware of the island's veneration of him. It wasn't until several years later that the British resident commissioner, John Champion, informed him, and the Prince duly sent a signed photograph of himself. Inspired by the gesture, the islanders sent back a traditional pig-killing club, known as a *nal-nal*. When another photograph was sent of the Prince in 1980, holding the club, it cemented their belief he was a holy man.

The people of Tanna worshiped the prince, believing him to be the "True Messiah."

THE GODLIKE PRINCE

While Prince Philip never visited the area again, in 2007, members of the tribe were invited to England and were given an audience with him. Gifts were exchanged and the islanders took home yet another photo for their collection. Two of Philip's children, Princess Anne and Prince Charles (now King Charles III), visited the island in 2014 and 2018 respectively, and when Prince Harry married Meghan Markle, the locals on Tanna threw a big party where they celebrated the wedding with dancing and feasting, and hoisted the Union Jack flag.

Those who worship the Prince believe his powers have directed global events such as the discovery of Osama bin Laden and the enabling of the USA's first Black president, Barack Obama. Shortly after the Prince retired from active duties, a dangerous cyclone threatened Tanna and the shrine set up by believers. Rather than take this as cause for concern, the tribespeople rejoiced in a clear signal from their deity that he was among them.

THE DEATH OF THE GOD

When the Prince died aged 99 in 2021, the villagers met over a long period to conduct ceremonial rites. Ritualistic dances, processions, and the displaying of photographs and memorabilia underlined their love for him. Symbols of great wealth such as yams, kava plants, and of course pigs were displayed as a sign of great mourning, and speeches were made by tribal leaders in remembrance. A message was sent to the Queen. Tribesmen believed that after the Prince's body had lain in rest and been buried at Windsor, his soul would return "to its spiritual home, the island of Tanna."

An anthropologist called Kirk Huffman, who has worked with the tribe, said that while they honored a period of mourning and continue to remember the Prince, their devotion has now turned to King Charles, who did also once come to their island.

CASE NOTES:
JOHN FRUM AND CARGO CULTS

The term "cargo cult" first appeared after World War II, as a Westernized explanation for the Melanesian tribes' long-held beliefs that their gods would send them ready-made goods. After the war, and the tribes' interaction with American troops who brought with them an array of equipment and supplies, these beliefs were strengthened on the island of Tanna.

John Frum was the name of one such deity. Beginning in the late 1930s, Melanesian islanders believed that this mythical American messiah would one day supply them with all their needs. Such was the very sudden abundance of material wealth that arrived with these Westerners, that when they left, locals presumed the goods were sent by the spirit world. To entice them back, they prayed to the gods that one day they might bring them everything they wanted, from cars to chocolate.

SYNANON

LOCATION:......... SANTA MONICA, CALIFORNIA,
USA

YEARS ACTIVE:....................................... 1958-91

FOUNDER:.......................... CHARLES DEDERICH

The group started as an innovative drug rehabilitation center before turning into a powerful cult that brainwashed members. Synanon was the brainchild of Charles Dederich, and at its peak had assets of $30 million, around 1,700 followers, and was feted by politicians and Hollywood stars. But then the group began to lash out at its opponents and plot their murders, becoming one of the most violent cults America had ever seen.

Dederich, 64, stands by his new wife, Ginny, at a Synanon branch in Marshall, California, in 1977.

Dederich was born in Toledo, Ohio, in March 1913, and endured a traumatic childhood. His father died in a car accident when he was four, and four years later, his younger brother died from influenza. In his late teens he dropped out of university and became an alcoholic. A bout of meningitis when he was 29 gave Dederich a permanent droopy eye and a facial tick. By 40 he had drifted through life, and when his second marriage ended, he traveled west and settled in Santa Monica, California. He finally found his calling when he attended his first Alcoholic Anonymous meeting in Santa Monica. He soon went to one every night as it gave him company and a platform to speak.

Dederich amassed his own followers and started to host meetings at his apartment three times a week, where he gave them his take on religion and psychology. He soon needed more space and in 1958 rented a storefront in Ocean Park where he spoke to around sixty-five followers at each meeting.

THE BIRTH OF SYNANON

After briefly calling his new organization "The Tender Loving Care Club," it was renamed "Synanon" when a member muddled up the words "symposium" and "seminar." Synanon began to offer a drug rehabilitation program in which fellow addicts and group members preached a mantra of "tough love." This was a confrontational therapy in which patients were routinely humiliated, and sometimes sleep-deprived and isolated. "One cannot get up until he's knocked down," Dederich said. At the heart was

"The Game," where recovering addicts and members sat in a circle for "truth-telling sessions." They would be verbally abused and have their secrets and weaknesses exposed. Anything was permitted, except violence.

Synanon was hailed as a revolutionary program, as most addicts had previously just been imprisoned without any help. *Life* magazine declared that the group offered "a tunnel back into the human race," while the senator from Connecticut, Thomas J. Dodd, said it could "lead the way in the future to an effective treatment for not only drug addicts but also criminals and juvenile delinquents."

Meanwhile, Dederich claimed that 80 percent of his patients recovered, and declared Synanon would become as famous as Coca Cola. In 1965 a Hollywood movie was released, eponymously titled *Synanon*, celebrating the work of the group with a fictionalized story. In the same year, after receiving a flurry of donations from wealthy businessmen and Hollywood actors, Synanon purchased three sites in Marin County, north of San Francisco.

"AN EXPERIMENTAL SOCIETY"

By 1968, Synanon announced a major change. Addicts would no longer "graduate" when cured of their addiction; instead they would remain inside the group and reject life on the outside. Non-addicts would also be welcomed to explore the group's teachings and new focus on psychotherapy. Dederich wanted to create his own utopia and what he called "an experimental society" in the communities he had created across California. He began to develop a God complex. "I am considered a megalomaniac nut," he acknowledged. "Of course this is true, but I'm not so crazy." He also said, "I am not bound by rules, I make the rules."

Members were encouraged to shave their heads, wear drab overalls, and live in the group's compounds. Any babies born to members were taken from them and raised in a "hatchery" before Dederich told them not to have any children at all, as they were a poor investment. Within days, his members had complied with him. Four abortions were performed, and 200 men underwent vasectomies. Dederich also declared that married couples should separate and find new partners for short "love matches," and within days 230 couples had filed for divorce.

In 1974, the group was officially recognized as a religion, and two years later had amassed such wealth that according to *Los Angeles Magazine* they owned 5,500 acres (22 square kilometers) of property, 200 cars, 400 motorcycles, 62 freight trucks, 20 boats, 12 airplanes, and an airstrip.

THE ENEMIES LIST

Around this time, the group's commitment to nonviolence was unceremoniously dropped. Beatings could now be handed out to members, and violence among them was encouraged. Synanon recruited a private security force and established a paramilitary group called the Imperial Marines, who practiced their own form of karate, "Syn-do." They armed themselves, spending $200,000 at a single gun store. "Our new religious posture is this: Don't mess with us. You can get killed dead," Dederich said.

Dederich kept his word. It was estimated his group launched violent attacks on over eighty people during the 1970s. A group of members attacked

A group of female Synanon followers in Oakland shaved their heads to show their devotion to the group, in February 1975.

trucker Ron Eidsen in his front yard in Badger on November 11, 1977, simply because he had cut in front of them on the road days earlier. A Marin County rancher was assaulted, another pistol-whipped, and two Black couples sitting in a car were beaten.

Synanon compiled an "enemies list" of individuals who had begun to ask questions. This included Jack Hurst, a former president of the group; Paul Morantz, an attorney and journalist who began to look into their affairs; and Paul Ritter, a former member who had grown disenchanted and left, although his wife and daughter remained inside, and his access to them was being restricted. As a warning to keep quiet, Hurst found his dog had been hung at his house, while on September 21, 1978, Ritter was beaten by two young men with wooden mallets and left with a fractured skull.

In June 1977, Morantz was approached for legal help by Ed Winn, whose wife Frances was held captive by Synanon for nine days. She had her head shaved and was taken from Santa Monica to another facility in Tomales Bay. Morantz began asking questions and discovered Synanon was not licensed to provide any treatment by the Department of Public Health. He eventually forced Synanon to release Frances Winn back to her husband.

Morantz was not content to walk away and dug deeper. He sued Synanon for kidnap and brainwashing on behalf of the Winns, who were awarded $300,000. Dederich was later recorded as saying, "Who is this guy Morantz? Why doesn't someone break his legs? We have a good thing here . . . we are not going to permit people, greedy lawyers, to destroy it." Synanon began to look into hiring a hit man to kill Morantz, but were put off by the cost of $10,000, and instead hatched a cheaper and altogether stranger plan (see Case Notes, opposite). In 1980, after the plan failed, Dederich pleaded no contest to conspiracy to commit Morantz's murder and was fined $10,000 and sentenced to five years of probation, on the condition that he permanently step away from Synanon. He died in February 1997 at the age of 83.

Without Dederich at the helm, Synanon slowly imploded; it had its tax-exempt status lifted and was ordered to pay back $17 million. In 1984, a court ruled the group had a "policy of terror and violence," and some members were guilty of embezzlement. Synanon was formally dissolved in 1991, although there remains an active branch in Germany.

Synanon members left a deadly rattlesnake inside Paul Morantz's mailbox to kill him.

CASE NOTES: RATTLESNAKE ATTACK

On October 11, 1977, Morantz was at his home in Pacific Palisades, outside Los Angeles, when he noticed a peculiar package in his mailbox. He placed his hand inside, felt an immediate jolt of pain, and screamed loudly as a rattlesnake sunk its fangs into him. The snake had had its rattler removed so it could launch a silent attack.

"Call the police! Call an ambulance! I've been bitten by a rattlesnake! It's Synanon! Synanon got me!" Morantz shouted as he ran back to his house. He spent six days in hospital but survived.

The day after the attack, police arrested two Synanon members, Joe Musico and Lance Kenton, for placing the snake in Morantz's mailbox. They were each jailed for a year. A month later, Los Angeles prosecutor John Watson and a squad of police officers arrived at Synanon's compound in Lake Havasu to arrest Dederich on a charge of conspiracy to commit murder.

ECKANKAR

LOCATION:....................NEVADA, CALIFORNIA,
AND MINNEAPOLIS, USA

YEARS ACTIVE:.................. 1965-PRESENT DAY

FOUNDER:............................. PAUL TWITCHELL

They chant "HU" in a long, drawn-out breath, as a love song to God, and their beliefs focus on the duality of the soul and body. Followers are taught that through this duality, a person can achieve self-realization. Eckankar draws on the philosophies of various religions and by promoting contemplation, meditation, singing, trance, and chanting, it promises to make your soul travel nearer to God. Eck teachings are said to be centuries old, but much of their past is shrouded in mystery.

In 1965, an American writer called Paul Twitchell claimed to be "The Mahanta" or the "Living ECK Master." He was born in Kentucky sometime between 1908 and 1922 (sources vary) and was fascinated by religion, spirituality, philosophy, and the occult. Having studied many religions, he joined a movement called Swami Premananda Giri's Self-Revelation Church of Absolute Monism.

Living in the church, Twitchell became heavily involved, editing the regular magazine. In 1955, an argument broke out between members which resulted in a fight, leading to Twitchell being arrested and thrown out of the group. Twitchell worked with Kirpal Singh, a spiritual master who introduced him to Surat Shabd yoga, a practice which claims to provide a path to spiritual completion under the guidance of a living master. Twitchell had also encountered the founder of Scientology, L. Ron Hubbard, in the late 1950s and became a member of Hubbard's church. Twitchell was once again very hands on, teaching classes and writing articles for magazines.

In the early 1960s, based in California, Twitchell wrote about his spiritual education, and much of his work centered around Eckankar. His new wife, Gail, encouraged him to use his knowledge to create a new religion. In October 1965, Eckankar (taken from Sanskrit and meaning "coworker of God") was registered as a company in the state of California.

Twitchell's Eckankar was originally based in Las Vegas and attracted a thousand followers in just three years, interested in its teachings about the soul, the "true self." Eckankar teaches that the true self can be experienced

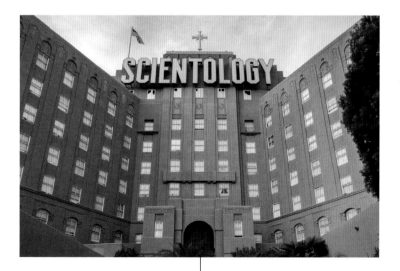

While it was said that he did not get on with Hubbard, Twitchell took a lot from Scientology.

The Temple of Eck in Chanhassen, Minnesota, was built in 1990, costing $8.2m.

away from the body, and that it is possible to be fully conscious and travel freely in "other planes of reality." Followers believe that it is through personal experiences that a person can naturally make their way to God, and that by shifting the emphasis of the body to the inner planes of existence, enlightenment can be found. With the right practices and teachings, followers believe a person's soul can exist and travel separately from the body and even from the mind. Eckankar uses mantras and chants to aid personal growth. The chanting of "HU" (pronounced like "hue," in a long, drawn-out breath) is their most important spiritual exercise. Eckists believe they will get closer to the divine being by singing it alone or in groups, while relieving stress, combatting grief, and helping to experience divine love.

Followers keep a dream diary, believing that dream travel is a gateway to "Soul Travel," a term created by Twitchell, giving a person the ability to move closer to God. Or as the Eckankar website puts it, "Broadening your viewpoint from even higher vantage points brings upliftment, problem-solving skills, and endless opportunity for spiritual adventure."

Twitchell was known as the "Living ECK Master" (LEM), a position that can only be held by a man, as followers believe only a man has the correct atom structure. When Twitchell died from a heart attack in 1971, he was succeeded by Darwin Gross. Gross moved the church to California, but in 1981, Harold Klemp claimed to be the LEM, and moved to Minnesota. While both men made the claim to be LEM for nearly ten years, today Klemp is the sole leader of Eckankar.

CONTROVERSY AND VIOLENCE

In 2006, Professor David Lane (see Case Notes, below) published a five-volume *Introduction to New and Alternative Religions in America* in which he accused Twitchell of plagiarism, giving examples of extracts from his writings that had been taken from a 1939 book called *The Path of Masters* by Julian Johnson. Harold Klemp has defended Twitchell's work, arguing that as "Master compiler," Twitchell "gathered the golden teachings that were scattered around the world and made them readily available to us."

Eckankar has always denied being a cult, arguing that they are not following a particular personality but a true religion.

CASE NOTES: PROFESSOR DAVID C. LANE

The professor who accused Paul Twitchell of plagiarism had long been skeptical of cults. Lane went on to write several books, including *The Making of a Spiritual Movement: The Untold Story of Paul Twitchell and Eckankar,* in which he attempts to expose the group as a fraudulent and tax-dodging cult.

Lane has gone on to write about many new religious movements and has been called "a cult-buster." According to the professor, he has been served with lawsuits, and members have written him hate mail, made death threats, and broken into his home. He remains adamant about certain religious groups, saying, "We use more discriminating intelligence when we buy a used car than when we buy a religion. Buying a used car, you at least look underneath the hood, hit the tires, maybe take it to a mechanic to check it out."

CHURCH OF BIBLE
UNDERSTANDING

LOCATION:... ALLENTOWN, PENNSYLVANIA, USA

YEARS ACTIVE:.................... 1973-PRESENT DAY

FOUNDER:............................. STEWART TRAILL

It all started in the 1970s: America was coming out of the revolutionary 1960s, the war in Vietnam was still raging, and mainstream religions had lost much of their support and influence. People were willing to listen and believe in spiritual alternatives. One such alternative was the Church of Bible Understanding, and at its helm was a man wanting to be heard. Was he offering real answers or was his motivation more sinister than this?

Stewart Traill was born in Quebec, Canada, in February 1936. His family moved to Pennsylvania when he was a boy, and having graduated high school, he dropped out of college. Said to be a bright student, Traill rejected the authority of teachers, and as a young man would describe himself as an atheist, but one with a keen interest in religion, initially in trying to prove the Bible wrong.

Traill used funds to finance many businesses, including the Olde Good Things.

A vacuum-cleaner repairman and salesman, married with five kids, Traill was said to have turned to Christianity in the late 1960s, stating that he could no longer disprove the religion's miracles. Into the 1970s and Traill gained the belief that he would lead an evangelical movement, writing in a diary that "Jesus was going to use him to reach the whole United States."

Having been expelled from his Pentecostal church, Traill began teaching and witnessing (telling people about Jesus), and in late 1973 he called a meeting. Around 250 people turned up. Traill called his movement "The Forever Family," and with his charismatic and "mesmerizing" personality, he gained considerable support. Young, energetic, and now seemingly organized, The Forever Family grew. They were discouraged from attending other group meetings, and Traill would consistently denigrate other Christian speakers. In 1976, based in Allentown, Pennsylvania, Trail changed their name to the Church of Bible Understanding.

"GET SMART, GET SAVED"

As his followers increased, Traill became increasingly manipulative, and members who had felt they were his equal became sidelined. Traill was the leader, and despite his domineering manner, such was his presence and charisma that word spread, and yet more followers joined the group. Traill would teach from the Old Testament, saying the New Testament was a "a bunch of flat statements of dos and don'ts." He had "Get Smart, Get Saved" badges made for himself and other members to wear. Traill would give Bible readings and lessons, but any debate about his understanding of the Bible and its scriptures was forbidden.

Raising the group's profile and membership numbers became the ex-salesman's key motivation. Members were sent out on the streets to persuade people (mainly young) to become Christians, and to join Traill's membership. This was done "to please Jesus," but it was clear that Traill was obsessed with numbers. Those not bringing their fair share of new people to him were accused of "faithlessness."

INFLUX OF WEALTH

Living a communal lifestyle, Traill's members would give any wages to the church and as it grew to 10,000 members and 1,110 communes, it is thought that he became a very wealthy man. Everything was put into the church's name to avoid paying taxes, and there were large corporate donations and government grants. Traill used the influx of money to start his own businesses, including a carpet-cleaning business called "Christian Brothers Carpet Cleaning" (later parodied in the hit comedy show, *Seinfeld*).Traill's children went to private school, and he purchased real estate in New York City. He acquired large warehouse spaces in which the growing membership were made to live, often in squalid conditions.

Life within the group became very isolated and some former members even felt they were "enslaved." Into his forties, Traill looked to indoctrinate young men and women, and while some believed they were doing the work of God, others felt they were being exploited. On one occasion, Traill allegedly ordered members to beat up his own son, who had been shoplifting.

Traill lived out his last days in a large mansion in South Florida, and despite turning on many of his members, stating that they "were helping the Antichrist," he was considered the church's pastor until he died in 2018. The church continues to be active today.

Evidence of the
tragic fire in the
Haitian orphanage
in February, 2020.

CASE NOTES: TRAGEDY IN HAITI

When Traill came to his members telling them that he was going to start
a charity looking after Haitian children, the initial response was positive.
Insiders, however, claimed later that it was a ruse to get more donations
and grants while avoiding tax.

Such was the lack of credibility and accountability, the orphanages in Haiti
under the church's control were said to be woefully sub-standard. In 2013,
an *Associated Press* report wrote, "Even though they claim in IRS filings to
be spending around $2.5 million annually, the home for boys and girls was so
dirty and overcrowded during recent inspections that the government said it
shouldn't remain open."

Despite that exposé, the orphanages continued to operate and in 2020, one
burned down, killing eighteen children and two adults. It was said to have been
started by candles used due to the facility's generator being faulty.

UNIVERSAL
MEDICINE

LOCATION:............................ AUSTRALIA AND UK

YEARS ACTIVE:..................... 1999-PRESENT DAY

FOUNDER:.............................. SERGE BENHAYON

A bankrupt tennis coach had an epiphany and founded a group
that an Australian court would brand "a socially harmful cult." Serge
Benhayon claims that he knows more than any scientist and convinces
followers to adhere to a bizarre set of rules and beliefs. Having
experienced one of Benhayon's "treatments," one woman launched
a campaign to expose the destructive nature of his organization.

In 2005, an acupuncturist called Esther Rockett, who had been feeling
stressed and run down, booked what was known as an "esoteric
massage." She visited Benhayon at one of his Universal Medicine
clinics in Goonellabah in northern New South Wales, Australia.

Uruguay-born Benhayon was a bankrupt tennis coach before becoming a cult leader.

Rockett returned twice more, but on her third visit began to feel uncomfortable when he suggested giving her "an ovarian reading," which she reluctantly consented to. It involved him putting his hands on her lower abdomen, close to her pubic area. "The first thing he said to me was, 'When you were five years old, a man in your life let you down,' before adding, 'As a teenager a man in your life tortured you'," which Rockett said were both "rubbish." As she told 7 News in Australia, "I walked out thinking, 'This guy's a predator.'"

Already signed up to attend one of the group's seminars the following weekend, Rockett decided to investigate his methods in more depth. There she found a conference room with sixty people who were asked to lie down in complete darkness before Benhayon gave a talk about spirituality. Some people began to scream and Benhayon said they could have been archangels who had been persecuted and raped in a previous life. "It was just the most horrible thing," Rockett said.

Rockett wanted to make a complaint about Benhayon but didn't know how, and so pushed it to the back of her mind until she read a newspaper article about him in 2012 which said his group's influence was steadily growing in Australia and they now had 2,000 followers. She began to hear more stories about Universal Medicine, including their questionable teachings, how they sought donations, and how they had altered the personality of some of their followers. She set up a website to document these complaints and actively campaign against the group.

In 2015, Rockett wrote a blog calling Benhayon a "cult leader" who was involved in a "scam," and said that his healing techniques were inappropriate, straying close to "molestation," which prompted Universal Medicine to sue her for defamation. The move would backfire spectacularly when the New South Wales Supreme Court ruled in Rockett's favor in October 2018 and declared, "Serge Benhayon is the leader of a socially harmful cult." It also ruled Benhayon was "a charlatan who makes fraudulent medical claims," who "exploits the followers of that group through his false and harmful teachings," and had "indecently touched" a number of his clients, including Rockett, in his treatment room.

A BATHROOM EPIPHANY

The landmark 2018 ruling finally stripped away any sheen of respectability the group had been operating under since Benhayon had founded the group nearly two decades earlier in 1999.

At that time, Benhayon, who was born in Uruguay but raised in Sydney, was still a bankrupt junior tennis coach in Alstonville, New South Wales. He claimed that one day he was sitting on the toilet when he suddenly had an epiphany, or what he called "an impress," that he was the reincarnation of the Italian painter and inventor Leonardo da Vinci. He began to call himself "an ascended master" and "one of the hierarchy," who was "connected

Benhayon believes he is the reincarnation of the Italian painter and inventor Leonardo da Vinci.

energetically" to an ancient lineage of "living wisdom" that included da Vinci and other leading figures. *The Sydney Morning Herald* reported some followers called him the "new Messiah."

Despite having no medical qualifications or background in science, Benhayon established Universal Medicine, which provided treatments, including esoteric breast massages, esoteric ovarian readings, chakra punctures, and esoteric connective tissue therapy. They provided a technique called Deeper Femaleness, which they claimed was "great for rape recovery."

The group also sold a course of programs to instruct their followers on how to lead a happier and healthier lifestyle. Benhayon has written several books and hosted workshops and seminars in which he espoused his views, which have been said by others to be a mixture of New Age philosophy, religion, and science fiction. Benhayon calls it "ageless wisdom."

"I know more than any scientist in my inner heart," Benhayon said in 2012. "I know everything about the universe and how it works. I can answer any question about any mystery in the world, any mystery in the universe."

BENHAYON'S TEACHINGS

At the heart of Benhayon's approach is his belief that the universe consists of "pranic" and "fiery" energy, and that the positive fiery energy found within the soul is often undermined by the negative pranic energy of the body, which can stop people fulfilling their potential.

Universal Medicine's followers are advised to go to bed at 9:00 p.m. and wake at 3:00 a.m., and if possible, only turn items in an counterclockwise direction. They should also avoid foods that may contain pranic energy, including gluten, dairy, potatoes, and carrots. Followers are warned that drinking alcohol can cause a break in their aura that allows evil to enter. The group have also suggested that their followers burp loudly to get rid of any evil spirits they might have inside their bodies.

Benhayon claims that when a man ejaculates inside a woman, she takes on all his bad energy. In addition, women are discouraged from playing sport as according to the group it thickens the vaginal wall, which makes it more difficult to have children.

The organization also believes that children with disabilities or those who have been sexually assaulted are being punished for mistakes committed in a previous life, when they could have been evil dictators or corrupt politicians. Benhayon said, "All autistic people are incarnate of former authority abuse over others, as are Down Syndrome, as are spastics, or any other disabled child."

Universal Medicine, who also have a branch in Somerset in the UK, has constantly denied they are a cult and listed the reasons why on their website, including: "a cult involves abnormal, sometimes secretive behavior, an all-powerful and controlling leader, dogma, and doctrines. On that basis Universal Medicine is anything but a cult"; "Students of Universal Medicine courses and workshops are completely free to come and go as they please"; "Teachings are in the form similar to any established learning institution"; and "There are no rituals, no mantras, and no exceptional practices."

"There is no brainwashing, it is about empowering people so they can be discerning," Benhayon said. "We don't keep people in a compound and we don't lock the doors, the doors are open."

Some of Universal Medicine's 2,000 followers at the Girl to Woman Festival in 2018.

CASE NOTES: FAMILIES TORN APART

An ongoing complaint about Universal Medicine has been that it has changed the personality of some of its followers, which has led to them being separated from their families.

"I think he's [Benhayon's] a master of separating people from their family and their friends. I think he creates doubt. He says, 'To change, you've got to leave behind these people,' and he splits up relationships," Matt Sutherland told a 7 News investigation in Australia when his partner Sarah left him and became involved in the group after doing their workshops.

In England, Anita Clifford became a follower of Benhayon's teachings and her family said it changed her. "She just completely went up in the clouds," sher daughter Kasha told 7 News. "You can't really describe how she changed, because she's not there as a person. It's like her whole brain's been switched off and she's got it replaced in the esoteric workshops. She's not who she was ten years ago."

In May 2020, the Court of Appeal in the UK ruled that a woman must make a "definitive break" from the group if she wanted to keep custody of her daughter. Lord Justice Peter Jackson said Universal Medicine had been a "pervasive source of ongoing harm to [the girl], emotionally and psychologically, and may make her vulnerable to eating disorders."

In an earlier hearing at the Central Family Court, Judge James Meston QC had said that Universal Medicine "is a cult with some potentially harmful and sinister elements."

FURTHER READING

Conley, Kevin. *Cults: Inside the World's Most Notorious Groups and Understanding the People Who Joined Them*. Gallery Books, 2022

Willis, Jim. *American Cults: Cabals, Corruption, and Charismatic Leaders*. Visible Ink Press, 2023

Chapter 1: Violence and Murder

Doyle, Clive. *A Journey to Waco: Autobiography of a Branch Davidian*. Rowman & Littlefield Publishers, 2012

Guinn, Jeff. *Manson: The Life and Times of Charles Manson*. Simon & Schuster, 2014

Guinn, Jeff. *The Road to Jonestown: Jim Jones and Peoples Temple*. Simon & Schuster, 2018

Guinn, Jeff. *Waco: David Koresh, the Branch Davidians, and a Legacy of Rage*. Simon & Schuster, 2023

Kimura, Rei. *Aum Shinrikyo—Japan's Unholy Secret*. Booksurge Publishing, 2003

Lewis, James R. *The Order of the Solar Temple: The Temple of Death* (Routledge New Religions). Routledge, 2006

Talty, Stephan. *Koresh: The True Story of David Koresh, the FBI, and the Tragedy at Waco*. Apollo, 2023

Tormey, Natacha. *Born into the Children of God: My Life in a Religious Sex Cult and My Struggle for Survival on the Outside*. Harper Elements, 2014

Usjyama, Rin. *Aum Shinrikyo and Religious Terrorism in Japanese Collective Memory (British Academy Monographs)*. OUP Oxford, 2002

Chapter 2: Nudism, Abuse, and Sexual Exploitation

Stille, Alexander. *The Sullivanians: Sex, Psychotherapy, and the Wild Life of an American Commune*. Farrar, Straus, and Giroux, 2023

Chapter 3: Fundamentalist Cults

Jeffs, Rachel. *Breaking Free: How I Escaped Polygamy, the FLDS Cult, and My Father, Warren Jeffs*. HarperCollins, 2018

Stalter Sasse, Cynthia and Murphy Widder, Peggy. *The Kirtland Massacre*. Kensington Publishing, 1992

Wall, Elissa and Pulitzer, Lisa. *Stolen Innocence: My Story of Growing Up in a Polygamous Sect, Becoming a Teenage Bride, and Breaking Free of Warren Jeffs*. HarperCollins, 2012

Yamamoto, J. Ismau. *Unification Church (Zondervan Guide to Cults & Religious Movements)*. Zondervan, 1995

Chapter 4: Conspiracy and New Age

Berman, Sarah. *Don't Call It a Cult: The Shocking Story of Keith Raniere and the Women of NXVIM*. Steerforth Press, 2021

Edmondson, Sarah. *Scarred: The True Story of How I Escaped NXIVM, the Cult that Bound My Life*. Chronicle Prism, 2019

Johnston, Chris. *The Family: The Shocking True Story of a Notorious Cult*. Scribe UK, 2016

King, George. *Contacts with the Gods from Space: Pathways to the New Millennium*. Aetherius Society, 1996

Morantz, Paul. *From Miracle to Madness: The True Story of Charles Dederich and Synanon*. Cresta Publications, 2015

Morantz, Paul and Lancaster, Hal. *Escape: My Life Long War Against Cult*. Cresta Publications, 2013

Spinks, John. *Cult Escape: My Journey to Freedom*. Independent, 2019

Zeller, Benjamin E. *Heaven's Gate: America's UFO Religion*. NYU Press, 2014

Chapter 5: Eccentric and Weird

Klemp, Harold. *Eckankar—Key to Dreams*. Eckankar, 2022

Sykes, Joe. *The Truth about Eckankar*. Independent, 2019

INDEX

A

Abe, Shinzo 95
Aetherius Society 128–33
Amin, Idi 51
AMORC 41
Angel's Landing 78–83
Ansar Pure Sufi 135
Ansaru Allah Community 135
Ant Hill Kids 72–7
Applewhite, Marshall 156–9
Asahara, Shoko 34–9
Ashtar Command 152
Atkins, Susan 30–1, 32–3
Aum Shinrikyo 34–9
Australia 140–5, 180–5
Avery family 110–13

B

Beausoleil, Bobby 30–1
Benhayon, Serge 180–5
Berg, David 66–71
Bistline, Faith 101
Black nationalism 134–9
Black Panthers 31, 32
blood sacrifice 108, 110–13
Bluntschly, Sharon 113
Boilard, Solange 76–7
Bonlieu, Edith 45
Book of Revelations
    17, 18, 157
Branch Davidians 16–21
Brand, Richard 113
branding 125, 127
Branham, William 23
Branson, Richard 124
Bray, Michael 63, 65
The Brethren 146–9
Bronfman, Clare and
    Sara 124
Brunner, Mary 29

C

Canada 41–5, 54–9, 72–7
cargo cults 165
Carlson, Amy 150–5
Carnes, Chip 105–7
Castillo, Jason 154–5
castration 157
Castro, Lou 78–83
children
    abuse by Dwight York
        135, 137–8
    abuse by Lou Castro
        80–1
    abuse by Warren Jeffs
        97, 98–101
    Ant Hill Kids 74–6
    Branch Davidians 19–21
    The Brethren 146–9
    Children of God 66–71
    Church of Bible
        Understanding
        orphanages 179
    Colonia Dignidad 22–7
    The Family 140–5
    FLDS 101
    Freedomites 56–7, 59
    Jonestown 14
    Love Has Won 153–5
    The Sullivanians 63, 65
    Synanon 168
Children of God 66–71
Chile 22–7
Church of Bible Understanding
    176–9
Cohen, Michael 64–5
Collins, Judy 62
Colonia Dignidad 22–7
conspiracy theories 152–3
Conyers, Michael 157
Crossfield, Bob 104

Culpepper, Joan 159
Currie, Kevin 110

D

David, Immanuel 107
Davis, Deborah 69
Dedrich, Charles 166–71
Delorme, Herman 42
DiAngelo, Rio 159
Di Mambro, Joseph 41–5
Dodd, Thomas J. 168
Dole, Bob 91
Doukhobors 55–7, 59
drug use 15, 29–32, 35, 37,
    141–2, 144, 153
Drury, Claudia 87
Dutoit family 43

E

Ebola 37
Eckankar 172–5
Edmondson, Sarah 125, 127
Edwards, Flor 68, 70
The Elder 146
end time beliefs
    Ant Hill Kids 73
    Aum Shinrikyo 37
    Branch Davidians 16–21
    The Brethren 146–9
    Children of God 66, 70–1
    The Family 142
    Movement for the RTCG
        48, 51
    Order of the Solar
        Temple 44
    True Russian Orthodox
        Church 114–19
extraterrestrials 128–33, 136,
    152, 156–9

F

Faith, Archeia 151
The Family 140–5
Family of David 107
Family International 71
Family of Love 70–1
financial exploitation
   Aum Shinrikyo 37
   Church of Bible
      Understanding 179–80
   The Family 144
   insurance fraud 80–3
   Kirtland Cult 108, 110
   NXIVM 123–4, 126
   Sarah Lawrence College
      Cult 84–7
   The Sullivanians 63–4
   Unification Church 95
Folger, Abigail 31
forced labor 13, 23–5, 27, 178
   NXIVM 126
   Sarah Lawrence College
      Cult 85
Ford, Gerald 33
The Forever Family 177
Freedomites 54–9
Freud, Sigmund 61
Fromme, Lynette 33
Frum, John 165
Frykowski, Wojciech 31
Fundamentalist Church of
   Latter-Day Saints 96–101

G

Galactic Federation of
   Light 152
The Garbage-Eaters 147–8
Giacobino, Alberto 44
God's People 55–6
Golden Way Foundation 41
Gomez, Patricia 79–81, 83
Goodwyn, Ron 78, 80–3
Gorbachev, Mikhail 92

Great-White Brotherhood
   142
Griffith, Mona 80, 82
Grogan, Steve 32
Gross, Darwin 175
Grunin, Eric 51
Guyana 13–14

H

Hak Ja Han 93, 94–5
Hamilton-Byrne, Anne 140–5
Heaven's Gate 156–9
Hempel, Winfried 24
Hikari No Wah 39
Hinman, Gary Allen 30–1
Hitler, Adolf 39
holograms 42
Hong, Nansook 94
Houteff, Victor 16–17
Howell, Vernon 17–18
Hubbard, L. Ron 173
Hughes, Brian 81–2
Huguenin, Thierry 42
Hurst, Jack 170
Huston family 80, 82–3

I

Ikazire, Paul 51
Imperial Marines 169

J

Japan 34–9, 95
Jeffs, Rulon 96–7
Jeffs, Warren 96–101
Johnson, Kathy 138
Johnson, Keith 112
Johnson, Raynor 141–2
Jones, Jim 10–15
Jonestown 13–14
Joslyn, Dick 158, 159
Jouret, Luc 41–5
Joy Rains 155
Joyu, Fumihiro 39

K

Kamagara, John 50
Kasabian, Linda 31, 33
Kasapurari, Joseph 50
Kashaku, Paulo 46–51
Kataribaabo, Dominic 48, 50
Kelley, Serena 69
Kenton, Lance 171
Kerik, Bernie 85
Kibwetere, Joseph 47–50
King, George 128–33
Kirtland Cult 108–13
Kishi, Nobusuke 95
Klemp, Harold 175
Knapp, Richard 105–7
Knights Templar 40, 41
Koresh, David 18–21
Kraft, Daniel 113
Krenwinkel, Patricia 31–3
Kuznetsov, Pyotr 114–19

L

LaBianca, Leon and
   Rosemary 32
Lafferty, Allen 104–6
Lafferty, Brenda 104–7
Lafferty, Erica 104–7
Lafferty, Ron and Dan 102–7
Lake, Dianne 29
Lamboy, Miguel 153, 155
Lane, David C. 175
Lavallée, Gabrielle 76–7
Leonardo da Vinci 182–3
Levin, Daniel 85
Long March 58–9
Lopez, Niki 137
Love Has Won 150–5
Low, Chloe 104–5
Luff, Ronald and Susan 113
Luffman, Dale 110
Lundgren, Alice 109, 113
Lundgren, Damon 112–13
Lundgren, Jeffrey 108–13

M

McGowan, Rose 68
McGrath, Daniel 83
Mack, Allison 126–7
McVeigh, Timothy 21
Manson Family 28–33
Mengele, Josef 27
Meyer, Adolf 61
militarization 26, 37–9
Moon, Sun Myung 90–5
Moore, Sarah 143, 145
Morantz, Paul 170–1
Mormon fundamentalists
    96–113
Moseley, Alan 130
Movement for the Restoration
    of the Ten Commandments
    of God 46–51
murders
    Angel's Landing 80–3
    Ant Hill Kids 76–7
    Aum Shinrikyo 34, 37–9
    Freedomites 58
    Kirtland Cult 108–13
    Manson Family 28, 30–3
    Movement for the RTCG
       49–51
    Order of the Solar Temple
       43–5
    Peoples Temple 14–15
    School of Prophets 102–5
    Synanon 170–1
Museveni, Yoweri 50
Musico, Joe 171
Mwerinde, Credonia 47, 50

N

Naiva, Jack 163
Netanyahu, Benjamin 94
Nettles, Bonnie 156–9
New Age cults 40–5, 122–59
Newton, Saul B. 60–5
nudism 57–8

Nugent, Paul 133
Nuwaubian Nation 134–9
NXIVM 122–7

O

Oklahoma bombing 21
Olivarez, Deborah 113
Operation Prayer
    Power 131–3
Operation Snatch 59
Order of the Solar
    Temple 40–5

P

Padilla, Sylvia 69, 71
Pappo, Marice 65
Parent, Steven 31
Pearce, Jane 61, 63
Penza Recluses 114–19
Peoples Temple 10–15
Phoenix, River and
    Joaquin 68
Pinochet, General Augusto
    22, 23, 25–7
Polanski, Roman 31
Pollock, Isabella 87
Pollock, Jackson 62
polygamy 62, 96–107
Price, Richard 62
Prince Philip Movement
    162–5

Q

QAnon 152, 153

R

Raniere, Keith 122–7
Rauff, Walter 27
Ray, Larry 84–7
Ritter, Paul 170
Roberts, Jimmie 146–9
Roberts Group Parents
    Network 149

Rockett, Esther 180–2
Roden, Benjamin 17
Roden, George 17–18
Roden, Lois 17–18
Rohan, Robert 136
Rosario, Santos 85, 86
Rosicrucianism 41
Rugambwa, Juvenal 48–9
Russian Orthodox Church
    God's People (Doukhobors)
       55–7, 59
    Old Believers 119
    True 114–19
Ryan, Leo 14

S

Sakamoto, Tsutsumi 37, 39
Salzman, Lauren 125, 126
Sarah Lawrence College
    Cult 84–7
sarin 34, 37–9
Schäfer, Paul 22–7
Schaffrick, Horst 27
School of Prophets 102–7
Scientology 173
Sebring, Jay 31
second coming
    Amy Carlson 153
    Anne Hamilton-Byrne
       141–3
    Charles Manson 30
    David Koresh 18–19, 21
    Luc Jouret 42
    Shoko Asahara 35
    Unification Church 91
    Victor Houteff 16, 17
Seven Seals 17, 18
Seventh-Day Adventist
    Church 17
sexual exploitation
    Angel's Landing 80–3
    Children of God 66–71
    Colonia Dignidad 22–7

David Koresh 19
FLDS 96–101
of Freedomite children 59
Jim Jones 15
Manson Family 29–33
NXIVM 122–7
Order of the Solar
    Temple 42
Sarah Lawrence College
    Cult 84–7
The Sullivanians 60–5
Universal Medicine 180–5
Shambhala 35
Silence Group 133
Sills, Howard 137–8
Singh, Kirpal 173
Sons of Freedom *See*
    Freedomites
South Korea 90–5
Spahn Ranch 30–3
Sprecher, Paul 62–5
Storgoff, Fanny 59
Stowe, Richard 104–5
suicides
    by the Movement for the
        RTCG 49–51
    Family of David 107
    Heaven's Gate 158–9
    Jonestown 14–15
    Order of the Solar
        Temple 43–5
The Sullivanians 60–5
Sullivan, Harry Stack 61
Swami Premananda Giri 172
Switzerland 41–5
Synanon 166–71

T
Tabachnik, Michel 44
Takahashi, Katsuya 39
Tama-Re 135, 136
Tanna 162–5
Tate, Sharon 31–2

Tender Loving Care Club 167
Thériault, Roch 72–7
Three Mile Island accident 64
Traill, Stewart 176–9
Trump, Donald 153
Twitchell, Paul 172–5

U
Uganda 46–51
Unification Church 90–5
United Kingdom 128–33
Universal Medicine 180–5

V
Vanguard 123–4
van Houten, Leslie 29, 32–3
Verigin, Peter V. 56–7, 58
violence
    Ant Hill Kids 72–7
    Colonia Dignidad 22–7
    Jonestown 14–15
    Sullivanians 64–5
    Synanon 166–71
    torture 22–7, 74–6
    Waco siege 17–21

W
Waco siege 17–21
Wall, Elissa 99
Watson, Tex 31, 33
WhiteEagle, Amerith 151–2
white supremacists 32, 42–3
Williams, Jerry 149
Williams, Robin 153
Wilson, Dennis 30
Winn, Frances 170
Winship, Gregory 113
women
    Angel's Landing 79–83
    Ant Hill Kids 74, 76–7
    Branch Davidians 19
    Children of God 66, 68–9
    The Family 140–5

FLDS 96–101
Kirtland Cult 110
Manson Family 28–33
NXIVM 125–7
submission to men
    23, 96–101
Unification Church 94

Y
Yamaguchi, Angel 71
York, Dwight 134–9
York, Jacob 138
Young, Michael 69

Z
Zerby, Karen 70–1

PICTURE CREDITS